INTRODUCING MELCHIZEDEK AND HIS KINGDOM

Sue Watkins

MelekShalom Publications

"The LORD has sworn and will not change his mind: 'You are a priest forever, in the order of Melchizedek.'"

Psalms 110:4

CONTENTS

Introduction

Genesis 14:18-20, "And Melchizedek king of Salem brought forth bread and wine, and he was the priest of the most high God. And he blessed him and said, 'Blessed be Abram of the most high God, possessor of heaven and earth, and blessed be the most high God, who has delivered your enemies into your hand.' And he (Abram) gave him (Melchizedek) tithes of all."

Hebrews 7:1-3. "For this Melchizedek, king of Salem, priest of the most high God, who met Abraham returning from the slaughter of the kings, and blessed him; to whom also Abraham gave a tenth part of all; first being by interpretation King of righteousness, and after that also King of Salem, which is King of peace; without father, without mother, without descent, having neither beginning of days, nor end of life; but made like unto the Son of God; abides a priest continually."

The above passage from Hebrews 7 appears to be stating that the Melchizedek of Genesis 14 was a supernatural king, one without a father or mother. However, that is a misconception. After examining the context, we find that the paternity/maternity, the genealogy, of that specific "priest," was not recorded in Genesis 14. Moses did not account for that priest's parentage because the priest was of the order of the "eternal priesthood." Note the phrasing: "... *he remains a priest continually."*

Clearly, this passage in *Hebrews* 7 states that the king/priest of Genesis 14 is of the order of the Melchizedek Priesthood. That order is eternal, and therefore its priests abide continually - *"like the Son of God."* In other words, the Melchizedekian order and its priests are eternally appointed.

So, essentially Hebrews 7 states that the Melchizedek of Genesis 14 was a forerunner to the Son of God, Yeshua.

My journey to this discovery began long ago. But it was not until after I retired and began devoting much of my time and energy to a lifelong desire to write that I understood the value of knowing the Hebrew language.

My intent was to write historical fiction with a biblical slant. However, my knowledge concerning the ancient past was limited. More precisely, I needed to know more about the era as it existed before Abraham was born. Therefore, research was necessary.

To garner information, I began reading the Apocrypha. As I searched for cultural clues, I noted a literary style that I began to call "Bible code." This unique code consisted of words and references relating to righteousness.

After rearranging many of these terms into Paleo Hebrew, I understood that Hebrew is multilayered as a written language. That eventually led me to realize how differently the ancients viewed the cosmos than we do, given our modern culture.

So, as I applied the grammatical concepts of Hebrew and sought the ancients' belief system, I began to understand the original intent of many of the ancient scrolls.

The more I studied the past, the more I unearthed errors in my personal awareness of biblical events. Let me be clear that the Bible should be read literally. Though, to stop there shortchanges the message. Ancient rabbis knew this. They taught that Scripture has four levels of understanding: 1) a literal meaning - *Peshet*; 2) a symbolic meaning - *Remez*; 3) a metaphoric sense - *Derash* and 4) a secret or hidden meaning - *Sod*. This type of study, or exegesis, is called PaRDeS – the acronym of these four.

Next came the realization that the central focus of Scripture concerns the government of the cosmos. Beginning with Genesis 1:1, God established a government, which shall be in place by the final amen of Revelation.

The deeper I dug into Scripture, searching for original intent in the Hebrew text, the clearer God's plan for establishing his government became. The ambiguity of my "worldview" dissipated. For the first time in my life, I understood why Jesus is called the King of kings. Many of the actions of the Bible's characters became understandable. Not only did I start to appreciate their deeds, but also the logic in their efforts.

Moses outlined God's plan when he recounted the Divine's creative acts; the formation of Adam, Noah, and the building of the ark, the calling of Abraham, the birth of Isaac, the life of Jacob, last but not least, the rise of Joseph.

The plan: Establish Melchizedek's kingdom. I have used this term, Melchizedek, for the sake of clarity in the presentation of this book. In that regard, I am in good company since the author of Hebrews also used it for the same purpose. Whoever wrote Hebrews went as far as to indicate Jesus came to Earth to officiate over the Melchizedek system.

The church lost this unique kingdom understanding when the church fathers diluted Yeshua's message with paganism. Consequently, by the end of the third century, all things Hebrew were abandoned, along with much of the schooling of the Prophets and the teachings of the Old Testament.

That, however, does not lessen the perception that Yeshua is the Melchizedek! And it is time for the church to have this foundational understanding again. The authority given to Yeshua is based upon the truth that he is "the King of kings and lord, over all lords." Because Yeshua is Melchizedek - every knee must bow to him.

The church, as *ekklēsía*, was called out of the world – to become citizens of the Melchizedek Kingdom. The world's government is "gentile," but the Melchizedek's government is Hebrew. And that, my friend, is why the author of Hebrews implied the meat of God's word is knowing Yeshua is the King of Righteousness.

Beginning with Adam and until the coming of Yeshua, there was a continuity of lineage. Adam's line passed forward a genealogy that belonged exclusively to the Melchizedek. Once I realized this, I grasped the importance of bloodline preservation and why Yahweh protected it. Only through that bloodline could the scepter be passed to Yeshua.

As the Son of God, his inheritance had to be free of curses. As the Son of Man, he received the scepter as a birthright. Yet, he received more, for his throne is the seat of all cosmic governments!

The Old Testament is the story of how the Melchizedek system was protected. The New Testament is the story of it being positioned. So, the Melchizedek Kingdom, more commonly known as the Kingdom of God or Kingdom of Heaven, is not "there" – it is here, in the most fundamental sense. It belongs to us; therefore, it is on the earth.

The Melchizedek scepter was passed from Adam to Seth, then through other kings until it rested with Noah before and after the flood. After Noah, the scepter was appointed to Shem, then Eber, before becoming Isaac's and Jacob's. Jacob contended for the Melchizedek scepter, protecting it until he could pass it to Judah for safekeeping. Hidden in Judah's bloodline until the time of the Messiah, the scepter became Yeshua's at the River Jordan, at his baptism, which was officiated by John the Baptist, a Zadok priest.

When Yeshua, as the Son of Man, became the final "eternal" Melchizedek, he fulfilled the promises. He did so as the last "Adam." The Old and New Testaments are in perfect harmony, and together they tell the story of the Melchizedek.

Luke 12:48, *"For unto whomsoever, much is given, of him, shall be much required."* Each generation was assigned a revelation. It is time for the Melchizedek Kingdom to spread throughout this realm. Therefore, I pray that the words on the following pages will bring insight and truth. Study - go deep into the *Sod*. Marvel at the Word of God. But more than all else, I pray that you see Yeshua as King - as Melchizedek, as your seated High Priest!

Chapter 1 - The Lineage

"So also, Christ glorified not Himself to be made a high priest; but He that said unto Him, 'Thou art my Son, today have I begotten thee.' As He said also in another place, 'Thou art a priest forever after the order of Melchizedek.'" Hebrews 5:5-6.

Melchizedek is not a name; it is a title. The term was formed as a declaration of allegiance to the rightful king. After Noah's flood, and the rise of Nimrod, the ancients began noting their affiliation with either Yahweh's anointed (Noah) or with his counterpart (Nimrod). If they aligned with Noah, they referred to him as the "king of righteousness" – the Melchizedek – primarily because he was anointed by Yahweh and, therefore, rightfully the king over all other kings.

This word, Melchizedek, occurs only in three books of the Bible. The first occurrence is Genesis 14 citing, the second Psalms 110. The third usage occurs in the New Testament book of Hebrews.

Hebrews builds its thesis on understanding Yeshua is the Messiah, and thus, the Melchizedek. The author of Hebrews based his argument using Psalms 110:1-4. *"The Lord* [Yahweh] *said to my Lord* [Adonai], *'Sit at My right hand till I make Your enemies Your footstool.'* [Yahweh] *shall send the rod of Your strength out of Zion. Rule in the midst of your enemies! Your people shall be volunteers in the day of your power; in the beauties of holiness, from the womb of the morning, you have the dew of your youth*. [Yahweh] *has sworn and will not relent, 'You are a priest forever according to the order of Melchizedek.'"*

The term, Melchizedek, is not in the text of Revelation 22:13. Nevertheless, the verse provides a foundational disclosure concerning the eternal king's infinite nature and superior authority. Yeshua states to John that he is the *"Alpha and the Omega, the Beginning and the End, the First and the Last."* In other words, he proclaims himself as the first and last letters of the Hebrew aleph-bet, and therefore, all that they represent.

"King of kings and Lord of lords" is an idiom that can only be associated with the Melchizedek - the appointed, anointed king/high priest of God's government.

Yeshua is and always has been the Melchizedek. That is clearly stated by Psalms 110:4. He is divine in nature yet chose to manifest in the flesh as a man that he might dwell among men. Consequently, Yeshua, dual-natured, as was Adam, was positioned by Yahweh to rule the cosmos from Earth.

Adam was also a spirit-being housed in human flesh; he was created in the "likeness" of God to represent Yahweh. Thus, Adam was divine royalty – enlivened in clay. But Adam did not rule the cosmos.

His soul was placed in human form, yet Adam was monogenic (one of a kind). That is the meaning of "only begotten" in Greek (*monogenes*).

Adam was the "first" man – Yeshua is the "last" – but since Adam typified Yeshua, Yeshua was *"THE FIRST AND THE LAST."*

There is an ancient teaching, which principally espouses two great powers exists. Both manifest in biblical writings as Yahweh. Church fathers viewed these two as Yeshua (pre-Incarnate Son of God) and Yahweh, God the Father.

Rather than digging deep into rabbinical teachings and mudding our understanding with difficult-to-follow theologies, it would be best at this juncture of our study to merely state the following: In the strictest sense, Adam represented the pre-incarnate Yeshua, not God the Father, Yahweh.

Psalms 110 could clearly be read as: *"The Lord* [Yahweh] *said to my Lord* [Adonai Yeshua] *..."*

1 Corinthians 15:45-47, *"And so, it is written* [in Genesis 2:7], *'The first man Adam was a spirit given life.' The last Adam, a spirit, quickens unto his appointment. However, the first was not* [supernatural] *but was natural, and after that, the* [supernatural] *man. The first man was taken from the clay of earth; the second from heaven."* (Author's translation.)

Yeshua came to serve humanity, but more, he came to re-align the earth with the Creator's eternal will. That meant it was incumbent upon him to come "like" a man so that humankind might relate to him – to interact with him. And so, he came as the Son of God, the Son of Man, that he might be accepted as humanity's King and High Priest, forever and ever.

As God, Yeshua owns the planet, in fact, all of Creation. But to claim that birthright, he had to be "of" mankind.

The Hebrew term most often translated as "earth" is 'erets. 'Erets, beyond being the name assigned to the planet, can mean land, territory, or the realm of existence given in this age to mankind.

'Erets was allocated to Adam. Essentially it is the kingdom Yahweh passed to his anointed king, instructing him to subdue it and have dominion over all its inhabitants.

Once we fully understand that concept, we can logically conclude that there are two sanctioned realms of existence. The first is the unseen cosmic divine sphere of the spirit world and the other 'erets, the physical world.

The unseen is overseen by a Divine Council, and Yahweh is their Superior Judge. Erets, however, belongs to the Melchizedek.

As you have probably surmised, I am skimming over many details. That is because I need to make this point: All is not "perfect." There is an ongoing war being waged in the unseen realms. That conflict is not being fought for the title deed to the unseen heavens. Instead, it is being fought for the seen realm of 'erets.

In the ancient past, governments were structured as "kingdoms" – meaning the king's domain. Consequently, the phrase "Kingdom of God" suggests God's domain, his divine government. That kingdom includes heaven and earth – the entire cosmos.

So, where does this position the adversary's kingdom? The fallen gods control the adversarial realm; they oversee the kingdom of darkness. More importantly, they are illegal actors who are outcasts; they abide outside God's realm. Yet they are warring to take the domain given to mankind.

Melek is the Hebrew word for king. *Tsedeq* translates as righteousness. When placed together, *Melek* and *tsedeq* form Melchizedek, loosely translating into "king of righteousness." More accurately, owing to the addition of a *yod,* which was placed between the two words, the literal translation is "my king is righteous."

A Melchizedek is both a king and a high priest. He governs the spirit as well as the physical. And because he does, he must be appointed by Yahweh. Therefore, his rule is "holy" – set apart unto Yahweh.

For an individual to be chosen as a candidate for the Melchizedek Priesthood, he had to prove his bloodline. That he was the Firstborn of a Firstborn, therefore a successor. Then offer testimony of his piousness. If those qualifications were met, then he could be appointed and anointed.

It might seem logical that the son born first to the royal family inherited that birthright. But that's not how it worked. Additional stipulations needed to be met. The primary requirement was righteousness within the heart, which only Yahweh knew if it existed. Outwardly, the postulate could not have blood upon his hands or be ignorant concerning the royal law of love. For these reasons, the prospective candidate sought Yahweh's approval that he might be accepted into the priesthood of the Firstborn.

As a priest, the Firstborn had to possess Yahweh's Spirit. In other words, he needed to be filled with wisdom that he might administer justice rightly. *"The Lord has sworn and will* *not relent, 'You are a priest forever According to the <u>order</u> of Melchizedek.'"* Psalms 110:4.

In Hebrew, the word "order" means "style of" or the "cause of." In Greek, the term is *taxis. Taxis* refers to the "succession of." That is to say, the sequential line of an arranged ordering. Hence, the phrase *"the order of Melchizedek"* simply refers to the continuous lineage associated with Melchizedek.

Next, note the Hebrew meaning of the word that was translated as "forever," it is ʿ*owlam*, which means concealed. My interpretation: *"You are a priest concealed in the lineage of Melchizedek."*

This understanding was an ah-ha moment for me; it caused me to realize the Melchizedek "order" began in Genesis. Suddenly I realized why the tracking of Yeshua's lineage was vital. He needed to be of the same bloodline as the Melchizedek, who appeared in Genesis 14.

So, like all others before him, Yeshua had to first prove his lineage, then he had to be publicly deemed righteous. Only after meeting those two requirements could, he be accepted into the priesthood. Received as righteous, by his Father, Yeshua was anointed and then positioned into that royal priesthood.

Once I grasped that concept, I realized why Yeshua had to undergo a baptism – why he had to enter the Jordan River and be anointed as 'the' Melchizedek. Additionally, I understood why there needed to be witnesses to hear the words of the Father and see Holy Spirit "come upon him."

It is crucial to connect Yeshua to the Melchizedek of Genesis 14. In turn, it becomes essential to identify the priest who met Abraham in the Valley of the Kings.

Genesis 14:18-20, *"Then Melchizedek, king of Salem, brought out bread and wine; he was the priest of God, Most High. And he blessed him* (Abram) *and said: 'Blessed be Abram of God Most High, Possessor of heaven and earth; and blessed be God Most High, who has delivered your enemies into your hand.' And he* (Abram) *gave him* (Melchizedek) *a tithe of all."*

Is it possible to assign a name to the Genesis' Melchizedek when the Bible has failed to do so?

As strange as it may seem, 2 Peter 2:4-5 provides a vital clue in identifying the Genesis 14 Melchizedek. *"For if God did not spare the angels who sinned but cast them down to hell and delivered them into chains of darkness, to be reserved for judgment; and did not spare the ancient world, but saved Noah, one of eight people, a preacher of righteousness, bringing in the flood on the world of the ungodly."*

Peter was not writing about the eight people on board the ark (i.e., Noah, his wife, their three sons, and three daughters-in-law).

Peter referred to Noah as one of eight preachers. On the ark, Noah was the only *"preacher of righteousness."* There is no record of Noah's wife, his sons, or daughters-in-law ever preaching.

Despite that, the word used by Peter in this text was not 'eight,' but 'eighth.' *Oktos* in Greek is the number eight. Peter used the word *ogdoos,* which means the eighth. 2

19

Peter 2:5 should read: 'but saved Noah, who was the eighth herald of righteousness.' Noah was the eighth herald (preacher) of righteousness, but what qualified Noah to proclaim divine truth?

Allow me to cut through many hours of research and simply state the bottom-line: Noah was a Melchizedek. He was the eighth Melchizedek from a line of succession, which began with Adam.

How did I conclude Noah was the eighth king since, per Genesis 5, there are ten generations from Adam to Noah?

Adam received an appointment and, consequentially, was anointed to serve as Earth's first Melchizedek. Seth, his son, was the second. Enosh became the third, Cainan the fourth, Mahalalel the fifth, Jared the sixth, Methuselah was the seventh, and Noah was the eighth. Note: we skipped over Enoch and Lamech.

Lamech never served as the king/high priest of 'erets; he died before Methuselah. So, Noah did not inherit from his father, Lamech, but became a "preacher of righteousness" upon Methuselah's death.

Methuselah died five days before the flood began. When Methuselah died, Noah became the king/high priest.

The seventh in line, Enoch, vanished from the Earth; he didn't die. He suddenly disappeared. Methuselah stepped into Enoch's position and assumed the duties of king/high priest.

Peter was correct; Noah was the eighth to herald righteousness globally. Genesis 6:9-10, *"Noah was a just man, perfect in his generations. Noah walked with God."*

"Perfect," as used in the preceding verse, meant Noah was undefiled. He was righteous in the eyes of Yahweh.

Pre-flood, there were eight kings/high priests. After the flood, only one of Noah's three sons was blessed. *"And he said, 'Blessed be the Lord God of Shem,'"* Genesis 9:26.

Shem was the Genesis 14 Melchizedek. He is the only one that could have met with Abram in the Valley of the Kings. Here are some additional facts that help substantiate our understanding:

1. Noah, at the time of the flood, was 600. Noah lived to be 950 years of age.
2. Shem lived to be 600, not dying until 2158 Anno Mundi (in the year of creation).
3. Abraham's birth - 1948 A.M. (290 years after the flood)
4. Noah was 892, and Shem 390 when Abraham was born.
5. When Noah died, Shem was 448, and Abraham was 58.

Most scholars consider the *Book of Jasher* a reliable historical source. The Bible refers to this scroll twice.

For that reason, we note that the Book of Jasher names Shem as the Melchizedek who met with Abraham: Chapter 16:11-12 "And Adonizedek king of Jerusalem, the same was Shem, went out with his men to meet Abram and his people, with bread and wine, and they remained together in the valley of Melech. And Adonizedek blessed Abram, and Abram gave him a tenth from all that he had brought from the spoil of his enemies, for Adonizedek was a priest before YAHWEH." (Adonizedek means the Lord of Righteousness. When officiating as high priest, the king was referred to as Adonizedek rather than Melchizedek.)

Shem's great-grandson, Eber, inherited the throne and its title when Shem died. After Eber's death, the title passed to Isaac. We know from biblical accounts that Jacob inherited the birthright from Isaac.

As Isaac's son, it was required of Jacob to receive his father's blessing! If Jacob had failed to receive Isaac's blessing, he would have never become the anointed Melchizedek.

The Melchizedek birthright was the birthright Jacob contended for, the one he was determined not to allow his brother Esau to have. However, Isaac wanted both sons to reign together. Yeshua's claim to the Melchizedek Kingdom would have been less than perfect if that had occurred. One of the other, either the king's throne or the "seat" belonging to the high priest, would have failed to be passed down to only one person.

Romans 9:11-13, *"Yet, before the twins were born or had done anything good or bad so that God's purpose in election might stand not by works but by Him who calls; she was told, 'The older will serve the younger.' Just as it is written: 'Jacob I loved, but Esau I hated.'"*

Abraham was grafted into the Melchizedek system, yet he never served as king/high priest. Even so, God positioned him as the "father" of Isaac, who would be king/high priest. And so, through covenant, Yahweh protected the Melchizedek system.

Still, we need to note some very interesting twists in this lineage that prove the supremacy of Yahweh.

Matthew provided Yeshua's "legal" genealogy, which came to him through Jewish law, reckoned through Joseph's family.

Matthew 1:1-17, *"A record of the genealogy of Jesus Christ, the son of David, the son of Abraham: Abraham was the father of Isaac, Isaac, the father of Jacob, Jacob the father of Judah and his brothers, Judah, the father of Perez and Zerah...Boaz, the father of Obed, whose mother was Ruth, Obed the father of Jesse, and Jesse, the father of King David. David was the father of Solomon, whose mother had been Uriah's wife, Solomon, the father of Rehoboam...Amon, the father of Josiah, and Josiah, the father of Jeconiah, and his brothers at the time of the exile to Babylon. After the exile to Babylon: Jeconiah was the father of Shealtiel, Shealtiel, the father of Zerubbabel...the father of Zadok, Zadok, the father of Akim, Akim, the father of Eliud, Eliud, the father of Eleazar, Eleazar, the father of Matthan, Matthan the father of Jacob, and Jacob the father of Joseph, the husband of Mary, of whom was born Jesus, who is called Christ. Thus, there were fourteen generations in all from Abraham to David, fourteen from David to the exile to Babylon, and fourteen from the exile to the Christ."*

Yeshua's mother, Mary, was a virgin. Hence, Yeshua had no DNA connection to Joseph's lineage. And so, Holy Spirit inspired Luke to provide Miriam's (Mary) family tree.

But before we look to Mary, note that a righteous connection to David was impossible through Joseph. That is why Holy Spirit provided Mary's genealogy through Luke's gospel. Luke connects Yeshua to King David by establishing Nathan, another of David's sons, as Mary's forefather. Which actually provides the only suitable pathway to David. For you see, there was a curse placed upon Jeconiah, a direct descendant of Solomon.

The curse upon the DNA (gene pool) of Jeconiah was recorded by Jeremiah 22:30, *"This is what the LORD says: 'Record this man as if childless, a man who will not prosper in his lifetime, <u>for none of his offspring will prosper, none will sit on the throne of David or rule anymore in Judah.</u>'"*

Next, we note that Yeshua was linked to Judah through David. Nevertheless, being of the Tribe of Judah, David was not a Levite. According to the law given to Moses, only Levites were permitted to serve as priests. However, a Melchizedek is both a king and a priest. So, since he was not a Levite, David could not serve Yahweh as a priest. This simply means that the lineage of Yeshua needed to go all the way back to the last "appointed" Melchizedek.

Also, David was not a Firstborn. 1 Samuel 16:12-13, *"And the Lord said, 'Arise, anoint him; for this is the one!' Then Samuel took the horn of oil and anointed him in the midst of his brothers, and the Spirit of the Lord came upon David from that day forward."*

As already stated, the Melchizedek birthright is an inherited title, typically going to the firstborn son. Whenever the firstborn failed to become the priest of his generation, another son was chosen. But by David's era, that practice had fallen away. But, in place in Jacob's day.

Jacob had twelve sons. The first of Jacob's sons was Rueben. Unfortunately, he could not qualify for the Melchizedek birthright because of his sexual misconduct with Jacob's concubine, Bilhah.

Jacob's second and third sons, Simeon, and Levi, were equally unqualified to possess his Melchizedek scepter. They both had blood on their hands, for they had exacted revenge for the rape of their sister, Dinah.

So, as we see in Genesis 49:1-33, Jacob placed the Melchizedek "scepter" with his fourth son, Judah.

"Reuben...you will no longer excel, for you went up onto your father's bed, my couch, and defiled it...Simeon and Levi are brothers--their swords are weapons of violence. Let me not enter their council, let me not join their assembly, for they have killed men in their anger and hamstrung oxen as they pleased. Cursed be their anger, so fierce, and their fury, so cruel!"

Judah... *"your brothers will praise you; your hand will be on the neck of your enemies; your father's sons will bow down to you. You are a lion's cub, O Judah; you return from the prey, my son. Like a lion, he crouches and lies down, like a lioness--who dares to rouse him? The scepter will not depart from Judah, nor the ruler's staff from between his feet, until he comes to whom it belongs, and the obedience of the nations is his."*

Jacob's blessing prophesied a divine appointment to travel through Judah to the Messiah.

So, Yeshua rightfully became the Melchizedek through Mary's ancestor, David, fulfilling the blessing Yahweh spoke over David.

Psalms 132:11, *"The LORD swore an oath to David, a sure oath that he will not revoke: 'One of your own descendants I will place on your throne-- if your sons keep my covenant and the statutes, I teach them, then their sons will sit on your throne forever and ever.' For the LORD has chosen Zion, he has desired it for his dwelling: 'This is my resting place forever and ever; here I will sit enthroned, for I have desired it— '"*

Chapter 2 - The Priesthood

1 Peter 2:9 "But you are a chosen generation, a royal priesthood, a holy nation, a peculiar people; that you should shew forth the praises of him who hath called you out of darkness into his marvelous light."

There are two Canonical priesthoods: the Melchizedek and the Aaronic.

Hebrews 7:11, *"Therefore, if perfection were through the Levitical priesthood (for under it the people received the law), what further need was there that another priest should rise according to the order of Melchizedek, and not be called according to the order of Aaron?"*

The Aaronic Priesthood did not exist until after the Israelites exited Egypt. And we note that only men of the Tribe of Levi were allowed to serve as priests. Which indicates this priesthood was temporarily positioned for a specified purpose. Especially considering the understanding that Yahweh had called the entire nation of Israel to serve Him as a royal priesthood.

Given these factors, the Aaronic (Levitical) Priesthood was limited. It could not achieve perfection since it was not an everlasting priesthood.

However, the Melchizedek Priesthood is everlasting; it is eternal!

When the Israelites crossed the Red Sea and entered the Sinai, they went that they might become the Melchizedek Priesthood, as Firstborns. That revelation, however, was not fully comprehended.

The Israelites lived in Egypt for four-plus generations. During that time, they had ceased to worship Yahweh exclusively. Egypt had tainted the "children" of Abraham, causing them to be worldly, no longer Hebrew. The Melchizedek promises made to the forefathers were forgotten. The ways of Abraham, Isaac, and Jacob were corrupted.

Yahweh, seeking a mediator to reconnect his people to the covenant of Adam, Noah, and Abraham, called Moses.

Moses was the one Hebrew in all of Egypt that was a member of a royal house. As the son of Pharaoh's daughter, he had learned the history of the world with the best scholars of his day. He was knowledgeable regarding the ways and beliefs of the ancients. It would be safe to assume Moses knew pre-flood history and thus, was familiar with the Melchizedek system.

Before Moses was born, a rebel had gained control of global civilization. That rebel was Nimrod. He usurped Noah as the Melchizedek and proclaimed himself the King of kings and Lord over all lords.

Egypt was a member-state of Nimrod's one-world system. Initially, co-governed by the pharaohs and Nimrod. Then some years later, after the fall of the Tower of Babel, Egypt became an independent nation, a force to be reckoned with. Still, as implied, Nimrod and all those that rose to preeminence while serving him did so illegally. They acted in rebellion against Yahweh, even opposing Yahweh long after Nimrod ceased to live.

To grasp the import of what I'm presenting, keep in mind the biblical concept that the "earth" is Yahweh's. After all, Yahweh is the one and only true God. Those who govern should do so because he appointed them. Yet, history is clear – that is not what occurred.

Next, keep in mind that the false religion/government implemented by Nimrod and his followers is "Babylon." It is a counter system. Babylon is ruled by the fallen gods.

Nimrod presented himself as the supreme ruler over all nations and functioned as their high priest. His system mimicked the Melchizedek system. Which effectually made him the king of all kings and lord over all priests. In other words, the ruler over the people of the earth. Essentially, he was the first Anti-Christ since he was "anti" (against) the one who was both anointed and appointed by Yahweh (Noah).

Moses understood the nuances of these things. He grasped the antagonistic relationship existing between the fallen gods and Yahweh. Clearly, Moses understood that Nimrod's rebellion against Noah exemplified the cosmic "war" of the gods. And knowing the history of Abram, that Yahweh called Abram to leave Ur (Babylon), he was aware that Yahweh had a greater purpose in mind for the children of Abraham.

Abram was told to leave Ur (Babylon) and return to the territory governed by Shem the Melchizedek.

Since Shem means "the name," Abram (Abraham) was instructed to go "live under the NAME." The "NAME" of Yahweh. Abram was to relinquish all association with Nimrod

(Babylon) by putting behind him the rule of the one *"who stood in the face of Yahweh and blasphemed,"* which is the meaning of the term Nimrod.

In obedience to Yahweh's directive, Abraham entered the land, which the Bible called Canaan. Soon after entering that land, Abraham <u>tithed</u> to Melchizedek. Hebrews 7:1-10, *"For this Melchizedek, king of Salem, priest of the Most High God, who met Abraham returning from the slaughter of the kings and blessed him, to whom also Abraham <u>gave a tenth part of all</u>, first being translated 'king of righteousness,' and then also, king of Salem, meaning 'king of peace,' without father, without mother, without genealogy, having neither beginning of days nor end of life, but made like the Son of God, remains a priest continually. Now consider how great this man was, to whom even the patriarch Abraham gave a tenth of the spoils. And indeed, those who are of the sons of Levi, who receive the priesthood, have a commandment to receive tithes from the people according to the law, that is, from their brethren, though they have come from the loins of Abraham; but he whose genealogy is not derived from them <u>received tithes</u> from Abraham and blessed him who had the promises. Now beyond all contradiction, the lesser is blessed by, the better. Here mortal men receive tithes, but there he receives them, of whom it is witnessed that he lives. Even Levi, who <u>receives tithes, paid tithes</u> through Abraham, so to speak, for he was still in the loins of his father when Melchizedek met him."*

The word tithe means "a tenth." The custom of giving and receiving a tenth was primarily for protection. The landowner (king) protected the "giver" of the tithe. Those who lived on the land paid the king a tribute (a tenth of their increase [harvest]). That tenth went into the king's storehouses and fed his armies.

This system was initially used to garner provision for the priest of the Firstborn Priesthood (Melchizedek). For it was taught that the tithe belonged to Yahweh. The giver affirmed his allegiance to Yahweh by filling the Melchizedek's storehouse.

In like manner, Abraham gave his tithe to Melchizedek, to Shem, that he might provide for his family's future protection. Abraham's tithe evidenced his loyalty and proved his dissociation from Nimrod. Abraham accepted Shem as his king and acknowledged him as a priest unto Yahweh by giving the tithe.

Abram was royalty; he was a son of Terah. Additionally, due to his great wealth, Abram was viewed by his contemporaries as a king. That is why the king of Sodom offered Abraham the spoils of war. The king of Sodom ignored the higher-ranking king - Melchizedek. Realizing the king of Sodom's motivation, Abraham said – no! Shem was the superior king. All tributes thus belonged to Shem.

So, in refusing to receive homage from the king of Sodom, Abram gave respect to Shem – to Yahweh!

Through that act, and by giving his tithe, Abraham entered into a covenant with the Melchizedek system.

Note that *"Abram said to the king of Sodom, 'I have raised my hand to the Lord, God Most High, the Possessor of heaven and earth,'"* Genesis 14:22-23.

Exodus 2:24-25: *"And God heard their groaning, and God remembered his covenant with Abraham, with Isaac, and with Jacob. And God looked upon the children of Israel, and God had respect unto them."* Yahweh, hearing groans, remembered Abraham, his tithe, and his pledge. Abram's tithe created a shield of protection, lasting protection not only for himself but for his descendants.

The word everlasting means: without an end. Since the Melchizedek system stands forever, the protection it affords is endless and everlasting. And so, Abraham's tithe not only established his loyalty, but it also obligated the Melchizedek Kingdom to protect him and his bloodline, forever and ever.

We usually think of the Abrahamic covenant as a blood-ratified covenant. However, no covenant between Yahweh and Abraham was blood-ratified until Abraham gave his tithe. Righteousness was not ascribed to Abraham until after he met with Shem. It was not until after Abraham's allegiance was established that heaven viewed him as righteous and recognized his commitment to Yahweh.

Abraham's tithe positioned him within the Kingdom and affected more than the events recorded by Genesis 14. His tithe purchased the birthright – it brought his house (present and future) into the succession of the Melchizedek.

The giving of Abraham's tithe was recorded in Yahweh's Book of Remembrance. Malachi 3:16, *"Then they that feared the Lord spoke often one to another, and the Lord harkened and heard it, <u>and a book of remembrance was written before him for them that feared the Lord, and that thought upon his name.</u>"*

"And God heard their groaning, <u>and God remembered his covenant with Abraham,</u> with Isaac, and with Jacob. And God

looked upon the children of Israel, and God had respect unto them," Exodus 2:24-25.

Yahweh heard the cries of Abraham's descendants. He then called for the scribes to read the record regarding Abraham. The scribes of heaven reminded Yahweh of Genesis 14:18-20. *"Then Melchizedek king of Salem brought out bread and wine;* (the elements of communion - the Lord's supper) *he was the priest of God Most High. And he blessed him* (Abraham) *and said: 'Blessed be Abram of God Most High, Possessor of heaven and earth; and blessed be God Most High, <u>who has delivered your enemies into your hand</u>.'"*

This blessing, spoken over Abraham by Shem, was forward-moving. It was a decree that would "<u>deliver</u> your enemies into your hand." The Hebrew word used is *"magan,"* meaning to function as a shield, as a Protector. Shem blessed Abram as a priest of El Elyon, the eternal God Supreme. In other words, the protection being offered was ongoing, as "eternal."

The words of any Melchizedek are weighty when spoken; they are reckoned as coming from Yahweh. So, like Yahweh, Melchizedek's words never fall to the ground, empty and unfulfilled.

Additionally, Shem offered Abram the communion elements – they participated in the aspects of a covenant.

So, what we must garner from these verses is this: The Melchizedek (the representative of Yahweh) approached Abraham so that they might have communion. He then blessed Abraham with the proclamation that he was "protected" by El Elyon. And at that point, Abraham gave a tithe. Do you see the exchange? Protection was offered – a tithe was given.

Abraham's past and current enemies, even those of the future, were delivered to him that day. A guarantee of lasting protection was rendered. So, four hundred years later, when his descendants cried out - Yahweh *remembered* the promise to Abraham!

Remembered is *zakar* in Hebrew. The letters of its spelling *zayin-kahf-reysh* paint a pictograph of "the weapon of cover belonging to the head." In other words, protection.

In that Yahweh remembered – meant he was once again offering protection.

Returning to Moses, we see him respond to Yahweh while standing in front of the burning bush. Yahweh appointed him as the spokesperson (mediator) to the Israelites - that they might possess the gates of their enemies. Essentially that was what was being offered to Abraham's offspring. Symbolically, Moses became both a priest and a matchmaker, a *Shadkhan*.

After Yahweh dealt with Pharaoh and the Israelites were in the wilderness on their way to the Promised Land, they camped at the base of Sinai's mountains. "*And Moses went up unto God, and the Lord called unto him out of the mountain, saying, 'Thus shall you say to the <u>house of Jacob</u>, and tell <u>the children of Israel</u>; you have seen what I did unto the Egyptians, and how I bore you on eagles' wings and brought you unto myself. Now, therefore, if you will obey my voice indeed, and keep my covenant, <u>then you shall be a peculiar treasure unto me above all people for all the earth is mine, and you shall be unto me a kingdom of priests and a</u>*

holy nation. These are the words which you shall speak unto the children of Israel.' And Moses came and called for the elders of the people and laid before their faces all these words which the Lord commanded him. And all the people answered together and said, 'All that the Lord hath spoken, we will do.' And Moses returned the words of the people unto the Lord," Exodus 19:3-8.

We should note that Yahweh asked that the "house of Jacob" become a kingdom of priests. Tribal identification did not matter. God desired to transform Abraham's descendants into a kingdom of royal priests, a nation set apart from all other nations as holy, belonging exclusively to Yahweh.

Yahweh told Pharaoh, through Moses, that the Israelites were HIS Firstborn. That indicates Yahweh wanted all of Abraham's offspring to serve Him as the Priesthood of the Firstborn, in other words, according to the Melchizedek system!

After climbing to the summit of Mount Horeb, where he met with Yahweh, Moses received this proposal. He then delivered this offer to the elders of all twelve tribes. They accepted on behalf of all the people.

The proposal's terms were clear: The "children of Israel" were to worship Yahweh as a "kingdom" of priests as a witness to all nations. They were to represent HIM by testifying to the world that Yahweh is the one and only true God.

Although the entire nation was to serve as priests, Yahweh promised the One prophesied to Adam and Abraham would come as the Melchizedek (king/high priest). First, however, the people as a nation had to commit to Yahweh. They had

35

to make HIM their God! They were to have no other gods, only Yahweh, and in return, Yahweh would take them unto himself as a treasured people, as a royal bride. Essentially, Yahweh would be their King/High Priest.

Moses accepted on behalf of the people a *ketubah* - a marriage covenant. It was written on a Tablet of Stone by Yahweh. After it was presented to the elders, they agreed to its terms (the Ten Commandments) and vowed... *'we do.'*

Interestingly, the word for stone in Hebrew is *eben. Eben* is spelled *aleph-bet-nun.* These three letters form a pictograph symbolizing - first son. The celestial stone Yahweh gave to Moses – represented Yeshua.

Moreover, ten represents "government." In that regard, we note that there were ten governmental rules written on the tablet received by Moses. Those ten rules were royal law, the same law that governs the Melchizedek Kingdom.

We should also view the Ten Commandments as the conditions to a covenant, for they were meant to serve as behavior standards.

The symbolism doesn't end there. Because the elders accepted the *ketubah*, a ratification ceremony was held (a marriage supper). That type of celebration was how marriage covenants were publically solidified.

Before attending the celebration, the bride would enter a *mikvah.* The *mikvah* ritual proclaimed her ceremonially cleansed and ready to exchange vows with her groom. After exchanging vows, the marriage supper commenced.

Likewise, this same ritual was mandated unto priests. Moses instructed the people to go into the *mikvah* (water baptism) for this reason. Exodus 19:10-12, *"Then the Lord* said to Moses, 'Go to the people and <u>consecrate them today</u> <u>and tomorrow and let them</u> <u>wash their clothes</u>. And let them be ready for the third day. For on the third day the Lord will come down upon Mount Sinai in the sight of all the people.'"

Allow me to restate an already provided principle: The Kingdom of God is the Melchizedek system.

Isaiah 9:6-7, *"For unto us a Child is born, unto us, a Son is given, a<u>nd the government will be upon His shoulder</u>. His name will be called Wonderful, Counselor, Mighty God, Everlasting Father, Prince of Peace. Of the increase of His government and peace, there will be no end. Upon the throne of David and over His kingdom, order it and establish it with judgment and justice from that time forward, even forever. The zeal of the Lord of hosts will perform this."*

Exodus 24:3 *"And Moses came and told the people all the words of the Lord, and all the judgments (decrees): and all the people answered with one voice, and said, 'All the words which the Lord has said will we do.'"*

Exodus 19:3 to 24:11 presents the *ketubah*, its acceptance, and the subsequent celebration. Exodus 24 outlines each step of the ratification process, which was, in fact, a blood-ratification ceremony. I should add that once a covenant is ratified, it can never be altered – in any manner. Not even an addendum clause may be added. A blood-ratified covenant is EVERLASTING!

Exodus 24:8, *"And Moses took the blood, sprinkled it on the people, and said, 'This is the blood of the covenant which the Lord has made with you according to all these words.'* And then, to celebrate, *"...they saw God, and they ate and drank,"* Exodus 24:11b.

During this initial proposal, acceptance, and ratification, the Levitical Priesthood did not exist. Also, note that the people were royal since they married cosmic royalty (the Divine God of the Cosmos). There is none more royal than Yahweh. Hence, Israel as a nation was regal; they were the Bride of the King of the Universe in every aspect!

Exodus 24:9-11, *"Then Moses went up, also Aaron, Nadab, and Abihu, and seventy of the elders of Israel, <u>and they saw the God of Israel.</u> And there was under His feet as it were a paved work of sapphire stone, and it was like the very heavens in its clarity. But on the nobles of the children of Israel, He did not lay His hand. <u>So, they saw God,</u> and they ate and drank."*

In these verses, the first "saw" is *ra'ah,* which means taking heed by looking upon; to discern. The second is *chazah,* which should be understood as "to contemplate."

Controversy surrounds the question of "who" they saw, for it is also written that no man can see God and live. So, let's delve into that uncertainty for a moment.

From the Hebrew text, we are given to understand they saw - *'elohiym.* Alan F. Segal wrote in *Two Powers in Heaven,* "rabbis acknowledge that God manifested Himself in two ways in the Bible."

Perhaps, what the elders and then the people saw was the entourage that always surrounds the appearance of Yahweh's throne. Or maybe they saw the pre-Incarnate Yeshua. I personally vote for the latter since that is who they were there to merge with. I am convinced that the Eternal Melchizedek was there at Sinai to make himself known to his Leah (the bride with the weak eyes).

I further propose that Moses and the elders entered into the "interdimensional" mountain of God. In other words, they were transported into the spirit realm.

But while Moses was on the summit with God (see Exodus 32), the bride, Israel, built a golden calf. She committed fornication with a fallen god.

"Moses saw that the people were running wild, and that Aaron had let them get out of control and so become a laughingstock to their enemies. So, he (Moses) stood at the camp entrance and said, 'Whoever is for the LORD, come to me.' And all the Levites rallied to him" Exodus 32:25-26.

Of the twelve tribes, only one tribe stood with Moses. Only the Levites aligned with him.

These events are filled with symbolism and much more than I can present fully in this setting. Nonetheless, the main takeaway necessary regarding this discussion is that Israel, as a nation, failed to give her loyalty to Yahweh as a bride. The Israelites committed adultery. Then to add insult to injury, none repented except the Levites.

Although Moses was born into the Tribe of Levi, that was not the primary reason why Yahweh chose him as a mediator. Moses was selected because he was committed to Yahweh.

The same is said in these verses regarding the "sons of Levi," they assembled behind Moses when he asked, "who is on the side of Yahweh?"

Again, we are asked to recognize the importance of loyalty, commitment, and allegiance. Yahweh chose the Tribe of Levi to be priests because of their show of loyalty.

On the other hand, Yahweh separated himself from the people due to their idolatry. The plan to form a royal priesthood could not move forward. It was suspended. Forced to wait upon the advent of the Messiah.

Afterward, a new marriage covenant was needed since the covenant, broken at Mount Horeb, was blood ratified. Not only was a different *ketubah* required, but also another bride. Until that could be arranged, a temporary fix was positioned.

So, all these things necessitated the Aaronic Priesthood. Yet, it was never meant to be anything other than a temporary fix. Hebrews 7:11-17, *"If perfection could have been attained through the Levitical Priesthood for on the basis of it the law was given to the people, why was there still need for another priest to come, one in the order of Melchizedek, not in the order of Aaron? For when there is a change of the priesthood, there must also be a change of the law (*ketubah*). He of whom these things are said belonged to a different tribe, and no one from that tribe has ever served at the altar. For it is clear that our Lord descended from Judah, and in regard to that tribe, Moses said nothing about priests. And what we have said is even more clear if another priest like Melchizedek appears, one who has become a priest not on the basis of a regulation as to his ancestry but on the basis of the power of an indestructible life."*

Matthew 11:12-13, *"From the days of John the Baptist until now, the kingdom of heaven has been forcefully advancing, and forceful men lay hold of it. For all the Prophets and the (*Levitical) *Law prophesied until John."*

Yeshua established a better covenant than the one Moses mediated. Instead of being written on tablets of stone, his covenant would be etched into the heart of every believer. The covenant Yeshua negotiated returned all humanity, not just the Israelites, to the royal law of Melchizedek. Also, it is not based upon human endeavors. It's guaranteed by HIS righteousness. It is executed by faith and maintained through obedience.

Galatians 3:18, "*For if the* inheritance *depends on the* (Levitical) *law, then it no longer depends on a promise; but* God in his grace gave it (the inheritance) *to Abraham through a promise."*

Galatians 3:6, *"Even as Abraham believed God, and it was accounted to him for righteousness."* Grace empowers the believer to live by faith. The same kind of faith that was accredited to Abraham as righteousness. Furthermore, access to Yahweh is given by grace. Grace does not mean that a believer has a license to break the law, any law, Levitical, or royal. However, now that Jesus has come, all may come to the Father through him - that is grace.

Grace has always been available, all the way back to Adam and Eve. Without grace, faith cannot work. Without trust in Yahweh's plan of provision and protection, achieving righteousness is impossible.

As the King of Righteousness, Yeshua opened a pathway unto "whosoever will" that they might obtain grace. Without faith in HIM, we cannot please God!

Galatians 3:19-25, *"What, then, was the purpose of the* (Levitical Priesthood) *law? It was added because of* transgressions (that is, the golden calf) *until the Seed to whom the promise* (of inheritance) *referred had come. The* (Levitical) *law was <u>put into effect through angels</u> by a mediator* (Moses)...*Is the* (Levitical) *law, therefore, opposed to the promises of God? Absolutely not! For if a law had been given that could impart life, then righteousness would certainly have come by the law. But the Scripture declares that the whole world is a prisoner of sin so that what was promised, being given through faith in Jesus Christ, might be given to those who believe. Before this faith came, we were held prisoners by the* (Levitical) *law, locked up until faith should be revealed. So, the* (Levitical) *law was put in charge to lead us to* (the Messiah - the One Anointed of Yahweh to be the Melchizedek) *Christ that we might be justified by faith* (in Him). *Now that faith has come, we are no longer under the supervision of the* (Levitical) *law."*

Ephesians 2:11-13, *"Therefore, remember that formerly you who are Gentiles by birth and called uncircumcised by those who call themselves the circumcision* (the Jews), *remember that at that time you were separate from* (the Messiah) *Christ, excluded from citizenship in Israel* (the house of royal rule) *and foreigners to the covenants of the promise (covenants regarding Yeshua's inheritance), without hope and without God in the world. But now in Christ Jesus, you who once were far away have been brought near through the blood of Christ."*

Chapter 3 - The Zadok

Psalms 110, "The LORD says to my Lord: 'sit at my right hand until I make your enemies a footstool for your feet.' The LORD will extend your mighty scepter from Zion; you will rule in the midst of your enemies. Your troops will be willing on your day of battle. Arrayed in holy majesty, from the womb of the dawn, you will receive the dew of your youth. The LORD has sworn and will not change his mind: 'You are a priest forever, in the order of Melchizedek.' The Lord is at your right hand; he will crush kings on the day of his wrath. He will judge the nations, heaping up the dead and crushing the rulers of the whole earth. He will drink from a brook beside the way; therefore, he will lift up his head."

Previously we discussed the lineage that Miriam (Mary) provided to Yeshua, stating that it allowed the Messiah to legally possess the Melchizedek's throne. The family tree of Miriam also connected Yeshua to the throne of Israel, David's throne. The problem is, seemingly, Yeshua did not sit upon either before his ascension. However, that assumption is not accurate. Allow me to explain.

Yeshua was given the Melchizedek Throne before Adam was created. He was assigned that position cosmically. Even so, Adam was appointed to represent Yeshua physically, only within 'erets.

The throne belonging to the Eternal Melchizedek has always belonged to Yeshua. Yet, because 'erets (earth) in its present state is physical, Adam was created with a terrestrial physical body.

So, Yeshua came as the Son of God to "become" the Son of Man. This simply means that Yeshua is "dual" natured – God Incarnate.

Essentially, we are proposing that due to the acts of the fallen gods, Yeshua was assigned to redeem the portion of Creation they corrupted. That is why he was the "lamb slain from the beginning."

The corrupted realm was 'erets, so heaven and earth were separated. Which made it necessary for Yeshua to enter the domain of 'erets that he might redeem Creation and Adam, of course since Adam had sinned.

Yahweh assigned Adam the dominion of 'erets because Adam was created as a "son of God." In like manner, Yeshua came to pay the penalty for Adam's sin, to redeem and restore 'erets to the Melchizedek throne.

In addition to being the son of God, Adam also represented mankind. Thus, Yeshua needed to symbolize "mankind" as the "second" Adam before going to the Cross and dying. Which made it necessary for the Son of God to become the Son of Man.

Revelation 19:11-16, "*Now I saw heaven opened, and behold, a white horse. And He who sat on him <u>was called Faithful and True, and in righteousness, He judges and makes war</u>. His eyes were like a flame of fire, and on His head were many crowns. <u>He had a name written that no one knew except Himself.</u> He was clothed with a robe dipped in blood, and <u>His name is called The Word of God</u>. And the armies in heaven, clothed in fine linen, white and clean,* *followed Him on white horses. Now out of His mouth goes a sharp sword that with it, He should strike the nations. And He Himself will rule them with a rod of iron. He Himself treads the winepress of the fierceness and wrath of Almighty God. And He has on His robe and <u>on His thigh a name written: KING OF KINGS AND LORD OF LORDS.</u>"*

Strong's Concordance NT#3686 states that *onoma* [on'-om-ah] translates as "name" literally or figuratively, representing authority and character.

The rider of the white horse was *"called Faithful and True"* and *"the Word of God."* John described him as one who *"judges and makes war."*

In biblical times, only kings executed judgments of war. This king of Revelation 19 did so *"in righteousness."* Both *"Faithful and True"* are synonyms of *tzedek* [righteousness]. Thus, the one who rode the white horse was the King of Righteousness – Melchizedek. Moreover, upon his garments was written *"King of kings and Lord of lords."* Thus, proving the Melchizedek John saw in his vision was the possessor of all authority.

Deuteronomy 10:15, *"For Yahweh, your God is God of gods and Lord of lords, the great God, mighty and awesome…,"*

1 Timothy 6:15-16, *"He who is the blessed and only Potentate, the King of kings and Lord of lords, who alone has immortality, dwelling in unapproachable light, whom no man has seen or can see, to whom be honor and everlasting power."*

Revelation 1:5, *"...Jesus Christ, the faithful witness, the firstborn from the dead, and the ruler over the kings of the earth...,"*

Matthew 28:15, *"And Jesus came and spoke to them, saying, 'All authority has been given to Me in heaven and on earth.'"*

"In the beginning, was the Word, and the Word was with God, and the Word was God." John began his gospel with two absolutes: 1) the Word of God entered *'erets* as the personification of prophecy, and 2) God and his Word are one.

Still, there is more, which links Adam to Yeshua. The name Adam means to show blood. Strong's OT #119, *adam* (aw-dam'); to show blood (in the face), i.e., flush or turn rosy.[1]

The one seated on the white horse was clothed with a robe dipped in blood, which indicated he had been wounded. However, since he had "blood," this also means that he was not a spirit.

Though the rider of the white horse wore garments covered in blood, they were also marked with the inscription: *King of kings and Lord of lords*. Thus, his vesture spoke, "calling" him the King – High Priest of *'Erets.*

Psalms 110 and Revelation 19 contain similar images. Both support the claim that Yeshua is the King of Righteousness, and both hint at what he is to do. Psalms 110 centers upon his role as eternal High Priest, and Revelation 19 upon him as the everlasting King.

---

1 Biblesoft's New Exhaustive Strong's Numbers and Concordance with Expanded Greek-Hebrew Dictionary. Copyright © 2006 Biblesoft, Inc., International Bible Translators.

Daniel 7:13-14, "*I was watching in the night visions, and behold, <u>One like the Son of Man</u>, coming with the clouds of heaven! He came to the Ancient of Days, and they brought Him near before Him. Then to Him was given dominion and glory and a kingdom that all peoples, nations, and languages should serve Him. His dominion is an everlasting dominion, which shall not pass away, and His kingdom the one which shall not be destroyed.*"

Scripture assures us that Yeshua came to lay hold of both the Melchizedek throne and the throne of King David. And we know that he accomplished that assignment. But how?

Yahweh watched Israel and then Judah commit unlawful acts. As the years came and went, the nation and its people strayed further and further from the truth. Abraham's descendants defiled themselves with the gods of darkness. Yahweh's chosen people sought to be like other nations. "*I gave faithless Israel her certificate of divorce and sent her away because of all her adulteries. Yet I saw that her unfaithful sister Judah had no fear; she also went out and committed adultery. Because Israel's immorality mattered so little to her, she defiled the land and committed adultery with stone and wood. Despite all this, her unfaithful sister Judah did not return to me with all her heart, but only in pretense,' declares the LORD,*" Jeremiah 3:8-10.

The structure (theocracy) that Yahweh instructed Moses to teach the Israelites became distorted. Instead of transforming them into righteous servants, it was used to lead them into the religious dogma of Judaism.

Essentially, the Aaronic Priesthood lost sight of Yahweh's supremacy and his demand for justice. Consequently, that priesthood failed both the people and Yahweh.

The priests and eventually the rulers of Israel, desiring global acceptance, were polarized as political factions. They argued the law with one another, and corruption spread like cancer. Politically contaminated, these rulers, motivated by their selfish agendas, seized every opportunity to push the people further onto paths leading to anguish. The blind led the blind, and they all stumbled, falling hopelessly into the proverbial pit of despair.

Again, God looked down and remembered! Once again, he remembered Abraham, Isaac, and Jacob. However, this time, Yahweh sent his Son, his only begotten Son, to restore all authority to the Throne of 'Erets. He sent the only one (Yeshua) who loved HIM (Yahweh) beyond measure. So much so he was entirely committed to the cause. So devoted that he would pay the price to reinstate all that had been stolen.

The time allocated to the Levitical Priesthood was expired. That meant a transference (return) to the Melchizedek Priesthood was authorized. To make that exchange, Yeshua needed a righteous priest of the Aaronic Priesthood to go with him to the *mikvah*.

To state this in simple terms, the "Son of God," as Yahweh's Firstborn (only begotten), came to the people of Earth as Adam's Redeemer. However, for it to be official, the people of 'erets needed to witness his appointment. That meant they needed to see his anointing as Yahweh's Firstborn.

Hebrews 7:11-8:1 *"If perfection could have been attained through the Levitical Priesthood (for on the basis of it the law was given to the people), why was there still need for another priest to come-one in the order of Melchizedek, not in the order of Aaron? For when there is a change of the priesthood, there must also be a change of the law. He of whom these things are said belonged to a different tribe, and no one from that tribe has ever served at the altar. For it is clear that our Lord descended from Judah, and in regard to that tribe, Moses said nothing about priests. And what we have said is even more clear if another priest like Melchizedek appears, one who has become a priest not on the basis of a regulation as to his ancestry but on the basis of the power of an indestructible life. For it is declared: 'You are a priest forever, in the order of Melchizedek.' The former regulation is set aside because it was weak and useless (for the law made nothing perfect), and a better hope is introduced, by which we draw near to God. And it was not without an oath! Others became priests without any oath, but he became a priest with an oath when God said to him: 'The Lord has sworn and will not change his mind; you are a priest forever.' Because of this oath, Jesus has become the guarantee of a better covenant. Now there have been many of those priests since death prevented them from continuing in office, but because Jesus lives forever, he has a permanent priesthood. Therefore, he is able to save completely those who come to God through him because he always lives to intercede for them. Such a high priest meets our need-one who is holy, blameless, pure, set apart from sinners, exalted above the heavens. Unlike the other high priests, he does not need to offer sacrifices day after day, first for his own sins and then for the sins of the people. He sacrificed for their sins once for all when he offered himself. For the law appoints as high priests, men who are weak; but the oath, which came after the law, appointed the Son, who has been made perfect forever."*

1 Peter 1:3-5 *"Blessed be the God and Father of our Lord Jesus Christ, who according to His abundant mercy <u>has begotten us again to a living hope through the resurrection of Jesus Christ from the dead</u>, to an inheritance incorruptible and undefiled and that does not fade away, reserved in heaven for you, who are kept by the power of God through faith for a salvation ready to be revealed in the last time."*

Revelation 1:8, *"I am the Alpha and the Omega, the Beginning and the End," says the Lord, "<u>who is</u> and <u>who was</u> and <u>who is to come, the Almighty</u>."*

As suggested by the term "almighty," God's sovereignty is absolute.

Yeshua was called upon to create a future without sin and death, thereby restoring absolute rule to the Kingdom of God. Essentially, Yeshua was to reverse the curse of death. Not only did Yeshua do this, what he accomplished cannot – ever – be undone!

Genesis 17:4-8, *"As for me, behold, my covenant is with you, and you shall be a father of many nations. No longer shall your name be called Abram, but your name shall be Abraham, for I have made you a father of many nations. I will make you exceedingly fruitful, <u>and I will make nations of you, and kings shall come from you</u>. And I will establish my covenant between you and me and your descendants after* *you in their generations, for an everlasting covenant, <u>to be God to you and your descendants after you.</u> Also, I <u>give to you and your descendants after you the land</u> in which you are a stranger, <u>all the land of Canaan,</u> as an everlasting possession; <u>and I will be their God</u>."*

The "land" promised to Abraham was more than a geographic location on a map. It was Eden. Yes, the Eden of Genesis 2. And according to the book of Revelation, that Eden shall return.

Let me state that another way. The Eden of Genesis 2 is cosmic. And it shall return after the millennia reign of the Messiah as the New Jerusalem. So, more was lost due to Adam's sin than immortality. Access to Eden was denied to mankind. In other words, ready access to the Kingdom was lost.

1 Corinthians 15:21-22, *"For since <u>by</u> man came death, by Man also came the resurrection of the dead. For as in Adam all die, even so in Christ, all shall be made alive."*

Romans 5:12-14, *"Therefore, just as sin entered the world through one man, and death through sin, and in this way, death came to all men, because all sinned, <u>for before the law was given, sin was in the world</u>. But sin is not taken into account <u>when there is no law. Nevertheless, death reigned from the time of Adam to the time of Moses,</u> even over those who did not sin by breaking a command, as did Adam, who was a pattern of the one to come."*

Luke 16:16-17, *"The<u> Law and the Prophets were proclaimed until John.</u> Since that time, the good news of the kingdom of God is being preached, and everyone is forcing his way into it."*

Matthew 11:12-13, *"From the days of John the Baptist until now, the kingdom of heaven has been forcefully advancing, and forceful men lay hold of it. For all the Prophets and the Law prophesied until John."*

What did Paul mean when he wrote, *"death reigned from Adam to Moses*?" What did Yeshua mean by the statement that the Law and the Prophets were proclaimed until John? What did he mean by *"the kingdom of heaven had been forcefully advancing?"*

By examining the Koine Greek of Roman 5:14, we discover that it is more than possible that Paul was depicting death as a high-ranking "spirit" who rules as a king. So, to paraphrase that verse: "Nevertheless, the rule of King Death was from Adam to Moses."

Even so, keep in mind the subject was the "law" (Torah), not death. Paul argued that sin was not attributed to each person individually until Moses' law was written. Before the law, transgressions were attributed to "all" humans simply because Adam had sinned.

Yeshua's statement that "the Law and the Prophets were proclaimed until John" supports Paul's argument.

That *"Law and the Prophets"* was the Bible. (Predominantly, the Old Testament. The Septuagint translation of Moses' writings and the Prophets' predictive writings.) Those scrolls prophesied the coming of the Messiah and established the justification for the changes he would bring as Melchizedek.

Luke 16:16 proclaims a switch in priesthoods came with John. In other words, with his assistance.

Hebrews 7:11-12, *"Therefore, if perfection were through the Levitical priesthood (for under it the people received the law), what further need was there that another priest should rise according to the order of Melchizedek, and not be called according to the order of Aaron? For the priesthood being changed, of necessity, there is also a change of the law."*

John facilitated the return of the Melchizedek system as a Levitical priest. Of course, he did so under the directive of Yeshua.

Yeshua's words, *"from the days of John the Baptist,"* referred to John's status within the Aaronic Priesthood. Simply stated: The time allotted to the Levitical law was over. It ended when Yeshua and John went into the Jordan River.

The Levitical era was over as the Melchizedekian order commenced. The "new" was moving forward with force – with violent words, strong words that catch or take hold of the Kingdom through energetic "proclamations."

To fully grasp this concept, we turn to Exodus 3:1-6. *"Now Moses was tending the flock of Jethro his father-in-law, the priest of Midian, and he led the flock to the far side of the desert and came to Horeb, the mountain of God* (Elohim). *There the angel of the LORD* (Yahweh) *appeared to him in flames of fire from within a bush. Moses saw that though the bush was on fire, it did not burn up. So, Moses thought, 'I will go over and see this strange sight--why the bush does not burn up.' When the LORD* (Yahweh) *saw that he had gone over to look, God called to him from within the bush, 'Moses! Moses!' And Moses said, 'Here I am.'*

"Do not come any closer,' God said. 'Take off your sandals, for the place where you are standing is holy ground.' Then he said, 'I am the God of your father, the God of Abraham, the God of Isaac, and the God of Jacob...'"

Note the command to take off *'your sandals'* (amad 'al adamah qodesh huw). Moses was instructed to remove his sandals to engage in a sacred transaction with Yahweh. The removal of his sandals was not just a holy act. It was also a legal transaction that signified the transference of property.

Malachi 4:5-6, *"Behold, I will send you Elijah the prophet before the coming of the great and dreadful day of the Lord. And he will turn [back] the hearts of the fathers to the children, and the hearts of the children to their fathers, lest I come and strike the earth with a curse."*

Yeshua said of John, *"...he is Elijah who is to come. He who has ears to hear, let him hear!"* Matthew 11:14-15

Before the Melchizedek Priesthood could be re-established, the "spirit of Elijah" had to come. The name Elijah translates as *"Eliyahu,"* meaning <u>Yah is God</u>.

Yahweh answered Moses when he asked, "What is His name? What shall I say to them?"₂ say, *"I AM WHO I AM."*₃

"Say, I am Yah, the את" – the Aleph-Tav – the first and the last!"

Moses met with Yah at the burning bush. He met with the "eternal" Melchizedek. He was instructed to take the "children of Abraham, Isaac, and Jacob" into the wilderness

---

2 Exodus 3:13

3 Exodus 3:14

so that they may become a "royal priesthood." Like Adam, Noah, and Abraham, Moses represented God and King.

Yet, the people Moses led out of the wilderness failed to become "royal" priests. Consequently, it was prophesied that the Spirit of Yah would come again, and the children would return to the "fathers," to the patriarchs, to Melchizedek's royal priesthood.

Mark 1:2-4, "*As it is written in the Prophets: 'Behold, I send My messenger before Your face, who will prepare Your way before You.' The voice of one crying in the wilderness: 'Prepare the way of the Lord; Make His paths straight.' John came baptizing in the wilderness and preaching a baptism of repentance for the remission of sins.*"

The "old" system was birthed in the wilderness – its purpose was to proclaim the "new." Repentance simply means to change or switch from one belief system to another. That is why John preached repentance. He came in the spirit of Elijah. The message he preached was meant to restore the "ways of the forefathers," Abraham, Isaac, and Jacob, back to their children.

Like the king, the primary responsibility of a high priest is governing. But he does so from within the temple, seated on a throne, as the highest sitting judge.

Zechariah 6:12-13, "*Then speak to him, saying, thus says the Lord of hosts, saying: 'Behold, the Man whose name is the BRANCH! From His place He shall branch out, and He shall build the temple of the Lord. Yes, He shall build the temple of the Lord. He shall bear the glory and shall sit and rule on His throne. So, He shall be a priest on His throne, and the counsel of peace shall be between them both.'*"

Before he could sit and decree judgments, the high priest first had to be ceremonially cleansed. That meant, among other things, he had to enter a *mikvah.*

According to Thayer's Greek Lexicon, the English word baptism comes from the Greek word *baptizó,* which means to cleanse by submerging in water until totally immersed. After leaving the *mikvah*, the priest robes himself with clean (sanctified) vestures.

This full submersion into water symbolized several things. Chiefly, the priest was submitted to Yahweh and dead to himself.

Aware that John the Immerser was at the Jordan River, Yeshua intentionally sought him out. The principal reason, John was a Zadok.

Zadok, צדוק or *Tzadok,* means righteous, justified.

The royal house of King David was attended by Zadok priests. In fact, the first high priest of Jerusalem's first temple was Zadok. Though he served during the reign of King Solomon, he began his service as a high priest while David was king.

The Zadoks traced their lineage to Eleazar, the son of Aaron. And as sons of Zadok, they continued to serve, throughout Israel's history, side by side with the royal house. As priests, they remained righteous and pious though other priestly lineages failed to do so.

Many of the Dead Sea Scrolls were written by the Zadoks. One of the Dead Sea Scrolls' fragments depicts "the sons of Zadok the Priest" as "the keepers of the covenant."

The Zadok priests of John's era left Jerusalem. They went out into the Judean desert because the priesthood serving the Second Temple was corrupt.

Ezekiel 44:15-17, *"But the priests, the Levites, the sons of Zadok, who kept the charge of my sanctuary when the children of Israel went astray from me, they shall come near me to minister to me; and they shall stand before me to offer me the fat and the blood," says the Lord God. "They shall enter my sanctuary, and they shall come near my table to minister to me, and they shall keep my charge. And it shall be, whenever they enter the gates of the inner court, that they shall put on linen garments; no wool shall come upon them while they minister within the gates of the inner court or within the house."*

Zadok, as noted, served as the first high priest of Solomon's temple. The first high priest of Herod's temple was also a Zadok, Yahusha ben Sie. He was serving at the time of Yeshua's birth. However, by the time Yeshua was positioned for his earthly ministry, the priests serving at Jerusalem did so at Rome's pleasure; they were appointed for political purposes. Thus, the Zadokites left, no longer facilitating Jerusalem's temple in any regard.

That a priest could purchase an appointment to Herod's temple and become a high priest through an association with Rome speaks volumes about the political climate of that day. The high priest was appointed by Herod, who fundamentally owned all the Jerusalem priests. He, of course, was an agent of Rome.

The Zadokites abandoned the temple, left it in the Pharisees and Sadducees' hands, went into the wilderness, and inhabited the Dead Sea area near Qumran to live a communal existence. Now, all these events happened before John reached adulthood and explain why it was written that John would *"come up out of the wilderness."*

Isaiah 40: 3-5, *"A voice of one calling: 'In the desert prepare the way for the LORD; <u>make straight in the wilderness a highway for our God</u>. Every valley shall be raised up, every mountain and hill made low; the rough ground shall become level, the rugged places a plain. And the glory of the LORD will be revealed, and all mankind together will see it. For the mouth of the LORD has spoken.'"*

Miriam, the mother of Yeshua, was a cousin to John's mother, Elizabeth. Elizabeth's husband, Zechariah, was a Zadok. Zechariah had served in Jerusalem's temple before John's birth. According to Abijah's priestly division (a Zadok line), Zechariah served in the temple when Gabriel appeared and announced John's birth. *"Do not be afraid, Zechariah; your prayer has been heard. Your wife Elizabeth will bear you a son, and you are to give him the name John. He will be a joy and delight to you, and many will rejoice because of his birth, for he will be great in the sight of the Lord. He is never to take wine or other fermented drink* (a Nazarite vow - which set apart one unto righteousness), *and he will be filled with the Holy Spirit* (the anointing of a high priest) *even from birth. Many of the people of Israel will he bring back to the Lord their God. And he will go on before the Lord, in the spirit and power of Elijah, to turn the hearts of the fathers to their children and the disobedient to the wisdom of the righteous* (note he will turn people to the wisdom of righteousness – to the King of Righteousness) *to make ready a people prepared for the Lord,"* Luke 1:13-17.

Luke 1:6, *"And they were <u>both</u> righteous [Zadok] before God, walking in all the commandments and ordinances of the Lord as blameless."*

John's parents were righteous – both from the Zadok lineage. Thus, in every regard, John was a Zadokite priest.

At the River Jordan, a Zadokite, anointed by Holy Spirit, led Yeshua into the *mikvah* – and garments were exchanged.

"John's clothes were made of camel's hair, and he had a leather belt around his waist. His food was locusts and wild honey. People went out to him from Jerusalem and all Judea and the whole region of the Jordan. Confessing their sins, they were baptized by him in the Jordan River. But when he saw many of the Pharisees and Sadducees coming to where he was baptizing, he said to them: 'You brood of vipers! Who warned you to flee from the coming wrath? Produce fruit in keeping with repentance. And do not think you can say to yourselves, 'We have Abraham as our father.' I tell you that out of these stones, God can raise up children for Abraham. The ax is already at the root of the trees, and every tree that does not produce good fruit will be cut down and thrown into the fire. I baptize you with water for repentance (to change how you think). *But after me will come one who is more powerful than I, whose sandals I am not fit to carry* (John was stating that it was not his place to write a new covenant, as Moses had after removing his sandals, but that the priest who came after him was qualified, far more qualified than Moses). *He will baptize you with the Holy Spirit and with fire.* (In other words, the One coming after him would administer

a mikvah like no other – a mikvah of fire, of Holy Spirit to purify.) *His winnowing fork is in his hand, and he will clear his threshing floor, gathering his wheat into the barn and burning up the chaff with unquenchable fire."*

"Then Jesus came from Galilee to the Jordan to be baptized by John. But John tried to deter him, saying, 'I need to be baptized by you, and do you come to me?' Jesus replied, 'Let it be so now; it is proper for us to do this to fulfill all righteousness.' Then John consented. As soon as Jesus was baptized, he went up out of the water. At that moment, heaven was opened, and he saw the Spirit of God descending like a dove and lighting on him. And a voice from heaven said, 'This is my Son, whom I love; with him, I am well pleased,'" Matthew 3:4-4:1.

John was groomed by the Holy Spirit for a specific assignment: That all righteousness might occur!

Note that John wore camel hair and a leather belt around his waist. John wore these to characterize his mission; he came in the spirit of Elijah. 2 Kings 1:8, *"A hairy man wearing a leather belt around his waist."* And he said, *"It is Elijah the Tishbite."*

At the Jordan, a voice from heaven said, *"This is my Son, whom I love; with him, I am well pleased."* This announcement was publicly made.

Essentially, this public declaration proclaimed Yeshua as Yahweh's Firstborn and blessed him accordingly. The blessing was both his "Father's Blessing" and God's. From that moment onward, Yeshua was legally positioned as the appointed and anointed Melchizedek of the physical realm, indicating Yeshua is the authorized King and High Priest of '*Erets*.

Yeshua would not officiate over the "sin" sacrifice at the Cross (the altar) until three years later. Still, the moment Yeshua stepped out of the Jordan River, he was Melchizedek – the King of Righteousness for the whole of Earth. More importantly, regarding the mission of his first advent, he became our High Priest! That is why the dove landed upon his shoulder. The dove represented Holy Spirit and the Melchizedek anointing!

Isaiah 22:22-23, *"The key of the house of David I will lay on his shoulder; so, he shall open, and no one shall shut, and he shall shut, and no one shall open. I will fasten him as a peg in a secure place, and he will become a glorious throne to his father's house."*

Chapter 4 - Caiaphas

Hebrews 10:1-14 "The (Levitical) *law is only a shadow of the good things that are coming-not the realities themselves. For this reason, it can never, by the same sacrifices repeated endlessly year after year, make perfect those who draw near to worship. If it could, would they not have stopped being offered? For the worshipers would have been cleansed once for all and would no longer have felt guilty for their sins. But those sacrifices are an annual reminder of sins because it is impossible for the blood of bulls and goats to take away sins. Therefore, when Christ came into the world, he said: 'Sacrifice and offering you did not desire, but a body you prepared for me; with burnt offerings and sin offerings you were not pleased.' Then I said, 'Here I am-it is written about me in the scroll - I have come to do your will, O God.' First, he said, 'Sacrifices and offerings, burnt offerings and sin offerings you did not desire, nor were you pleased with them.' Although the law required them to be made. Then he* (Yeshua) *said, 'Here I am, I have come to do your will.' He set aside the first to establish the second. And by that will, we have been made holy through the sacrifice of the body of Jesus Christ once for all. Day after day, every* (Levitical) *priest stands and performs his religious duties; again and again, he offers the same sacrifices, which can never take away sins. But when this priest* (Yeshua) *had offered for all time one sacrifice for sins, he sat down at the right hand of*

God. Since that time, he waits for his enemies to be made his footstool because by one sacrifice he has made perfect forever those who are being made holy."

Yeshua came to reinstate the Melchizedek Kingdom. However, as he traversed Judea ministering to the people, he carefully guarded the whole sum of that understanding from his friends as well as foes. The danger of his mission being prematurely ended by the Pharisees was at substantial risk. So, he kept his enemies guessing and friends wondering if he was the "true" Messiah as they listened to the truth he spoke in parables.

Yeshua spoke of his kingdom, but it is unlikely it entered anyone's imagination initially he was the promised Melchizedek. Most, if not all, who believed him, thought he spoke only about David's throne – not about the throne of the whole of 'erets.

Yeshua released his kingdom for three years, although only a handful realized that was what he was doing. And I doubt those few saw the whole of his mission. Crowds sought him, but make no mistake, it was not because they acknowledged him as the Melchizedek. They sought his miracles. Recognizing that he spoke with "great authority," the people quickly gathered about him whenever he and his disciples entered a village. They wanted to see what he would do next. And yes, they came bringing the sick or those possessed by demons; some even brought their dead, but they came for the miracles

Then at Passover during that third year, Yeshua made his way from Galilee to Jerusalem. The month was Nissan, and the year 32 A D.

Rumors raged. The Essenes were teaching it was time for the Messiah to be revealed. Their message filled the people with hope. Judea's citizenry, weary with the corruption inside the Jerusalem Temple and its priests, were seeking their long-waited promised Messiah.

However, they wanted a king like David – a warrior. They wanted their Messiah to bring down the Roman "giants," as David had Goliath. And more than anything, they wanted self-autonomy, which meant he would need to restore the Kingdom of Israel. However, Yeshua had not come as Melchizedek to restore the physical; he came to "restore" the spiritual. Primarily, Yeshua sought to be accepted as their High Priest.

A few days before Passover, Yeshua raised Lazarus from the dead. He did this because "his" appointed time had come. It was time to reveal his Divine mission to the "spirit" entities of the underworld, primarily to the Spirit of Death. And as expected, the miraculous resurrection of Lazarus caused that Lord of Sheol to suspect Yeshua was more than a want-a-be "messiah."

The underworld king realized Yeshua's authority was far more reaching than he had previously understood. The likelihood that Yeshua was "THE" Messiah, the One for which the Jews longed, was real.

John 11:4, *"When Jesus heard that, He said, 'This sickness is not unto death, but for the glory of God, that the Son of God may be glorified through it.'"*

John 11:14-15, *"Then Jesus said to them plainly, 'Lazarus is dead. And I am glad for your sakes that I was not there <u>that you may believe</u>. Nevertheless, let us go to him.'"*

John 11:40-44, *"Jesus said to her, 'Did I not say to you that if you would believe you would see the glory of God?' Then they took away the stone from the place where the dead man was lying. And Jesus lifted up His eyes and said, 'Father, I thank You that You have heard Me. And I know that You always hear Me, but because of the people who are standing by I said this, <u>that they may believe that You sent Me</u>.' Now, when He had said these things, He cried with a loud voice, 'Lazarus, come forth!' And he who had died came out bound hand and foot with graveclothes, and his face was wrapped with a cloth. Jesus said to them, 'Loose him, and let him go.'"*

Lazarus had been dead for four days. A human body begins to decay quickly; decay is entirely active by day four. However, Yeshua was dealing with the spirit realm, not the physical. Yeshua called to Lazarus, who was in the underworld. The sound of his voice sped past the grave, down to the netherworld, reaching the soul of Lazarus.

Yeshua's words had the effect of commanding the Lord of the Dead to open the tomb and allow Lazarus to return to the land of the living. That command stopped death and reversed decay. Only one of superior authority could command matter to react like that.

Note: Yeshua's authority was over Death, indicating he possessed "cosmic" authority. This matter went beyond the reach of those who sat in the Sanhedrin, Jerusalem, or even Rome. Yeshua demanded that the universe recognize and submit to his God-given Divine authority. However, that truth was not noted by the Pharisees. They only saw the danger in the people accepting this "man" as their Messiah. Which meant he threatened their authority.

When the news of this miracle reached ordinary people, their hope rose to great heights; Yeshua of Nazareth would be their Liberator. As the news of the resurrection spread, another problem arose, for not only did the average person on the street hear of the miracle, but the temple priests also heard.

Immediately upon hearing of this resurrection, the Pharisees called for a meeting of the Sanhedrin. Something had to be done to stop this Yeshua of Nazareth. That Yeshua could raise the dead was a problem – for political reasons. The crowds he attracted would be interpreted by Rome as a sign that the Sanhedrin Council was unable to control their people.

The Sanhedrin was the legislative body that officiated over all Jerusalem's internal affairs, functioning according to rabbinic tradition. But what concerned the Pharisees had nothing to do with the law; they were worried about their livelihood.

After presenting their case to the Sanhedrin, the Pharisees persuaded the body politic to conspire against the man they identified as Yeshua of Nazareth. They requested a directive that provided the basis for arresting Yeshua. But then Caiaphas, the high priest, stood. He addressed those in attendance by saying, "You might understand the problem, but you haven't reached the solution! Having this Yeshua of Nazareth to submit to us is not enough. He, as one, should die. Only one should die. Forbid the whole nation should perish because Rome is agitated by this rebel."

After considering Caiaphas' logic, the Pharisees agreed that a charge to arrest was not enough. However, the approaching Passover Feast was problematic. To try and then convict a prisoner at Passover was legally impossible. There existed in their law a strict ban against trying anyone while a high holy feast was underway. Knowing that the law had dominance over their need to act, the Sanhedrin, in turn, made it a priority to find Yeshua. He was to be arrested, held secretly, and then when convenient, be tried before the court.

So, an order went forth from the chief priests, stating that they should report it if anyone had any information about Yeshua's whereabouts.

Knowing all these things, Yeshua withdrew to a region near the desert, to a village called Ephraim. He stayed there with his disciples until it became compulsory that they leave for Jerusalem. Like all other able-bodied men of Jewish descent, Yeshua and his disciples were obliged to go to Jerusalem to observe Passover.

On the lookout for Yeshua, Pharisees stood on the parapets of the entrances into Jerusalem. Standing over the crowds, they watched all who streamed into the city. The multitudes were vast, yet someone spotted Yeshua. The word of the sighting quickly spread as people began to scream, "Yeshua is coming!"

Moving as one, the crowd rushed the gate, hoping to catch a glimpse of the Miracle Worker as he entered the city.

Waving palm branches was a part of the Passover celebration, so everyone carried a palm branch since tradition demanded they do so. Someone in the crowd got an idea, which he immediately shared. He incited the people to make a palm-lined pathway for Yeshua to enter the city.

Someone offered a young donkey to Yeshua that he might ride it into the city. Holding their palm branches above the road, the people waved them back and forth to celebrate Yeshua as he neared the City of David. Singing and shouting, they honored him with "*Hallel - Hallel.*"

Whether anyone in the crowd was aware of what was happening is unclear. Nonetheless, Yeshua rode the donkey down the opened path and through the gates.

These things were not happenstance but fulfilled predictive proclamations that prophesied Melchizedek would enter the city to bring peace. However, they happen so that peace between Yahweh and mankind would exist. Not a peace between Jerusalem and Rome.

As Yeshua entered the gate, a shout went forth from the crowd, "Hosanna! Blessed is he who comes in the name of Yahweh! Blessed is the King of Israel!"

The protocol for a king to be installed as the ruler of Israel required the following:

1) He was "nominated" – meaning he was appointed.
2) Yahweh's approval was sought.
3) An anointing ceremony was publicly held.
4) Then, on Rosh Hashanah, not at Passover, he was crowned.

Although the crowd cried out, calling him "King of Israel," what they were doing was fulfilling prophecy, not crowning a king. Zechariah 9:9, *"Do not be afraid, O Daughter of Zion; see, your king is coming, seated on a donkey's colt."*

On that fateful Passover, King Yeshua, as the Prince of God who will someday be ceremoniously seated in Jerusalem, upon Melchizedek's eternal throne, entered the City of David.

Standing on the city walls, the Pharisees, who watched the procession, said to each other, *"See, the entire world seeks him!"* (John 12:19).

Yeshua, however, turned to his disciples and remarked, "The hour has come for the Son of Man to be glorified...my heart is troubled, and what shall I say? 'Father, save me from this hour?' No, it was for this very reason I came to this hour. So, 'Father, glorify your name!'"

At that moment, a voice from heaven was heard by those who stood nearby, saying, "I have glorified it and will glorify it again."

Many in the crowd could not distinguish the origin of those words. Some thought they heard a voice, but others believed it had thundered. Others proclaimed, "no, an angel spoke."

Yeshua shook his head and informed all, "The Voice you heard was for your benefit, not mine. That you might know and understand that it is now time for judgment to come upon the world. <u>Now the prince of this world will be driven out.</u> But, when I am lifted from the earth, I will draw all men to myself."

Let's pause the retelling of these events to better understand Yeshua's words. Note those I've underlined from John 12: 30-32. They are fascinating. *"Jesus answered and said, 'This voice did not come because of me, but for your* sake. _Now is the judgment of this world; now, the ruler of this world will be cast out_. And, if I am lifted up from the earth, I will draw _all peoples_ to Myself.'"

Yeshua stated that the "god" of the age, probably the same one who entered the Garden of Eden and deceived Eve, was cast down.

I've paraphrased for you Yeshua's words: "Henceforth, by the tribunal decision of the Divine Council, the archon of the _cosmos_ is driven out. Henceforth, he is ejected from '_erets._"

The word _cosmos_ has a dual meaning. In a broad sense, it means the entire world, but in the more narrow sense, it means "order."

Speaking in the present tense, not of the future, Yeshua was stating prophecy had intersected with time. Waiting for him upon the Cross were promises yet unfulfilled. Those promises were made in Eden. But, at last, it was time to fulfill them!

You see, at that moment, the Creator's voice penetrated through all atmospheric interference to decree Yeshua, as Melchizedek had entered Zion. Psalms 2:6 was in the process of fulfillment, _"Yet I have set my King on my holy hill of Zion."_ Are you still seated? I hope not. I hope you are up dancing a jig!

To summarize the words the Creator spoke in John 12, "Because you came in my name, you carry my glory, and therefore, you cannot fail in your mission!"

Later, after his Father's propitious proclamation, Yeshua and his disciples sat down for the Passover Seder. He took the bread, blessed it, and broke it. Then gave it to the disciples, saying, "Take, eat; this is my body." Then took the cup, gave thanks, then passed it, saying, "Drink from it, all of you. For this is my blood, the blood that ratifies the new *ketubah,* which we now share. It is my blood, which is shed for many, for the remission of sin. However, I will not drink of the fourth cup, not now, not at this Seder, but I will drink it, with you, when my Father's kingdom has come to *'erets* once again, and for all times."

That Passover Seder was more than a celebration of remembrance concerning the Exodus; it ratified the *ketubah* Yeshua offered to his disciples. He followed a pattern, long-established, that was used to extend a proposal of marriage between two families. Yeshua asked his disciples to accept this proposal on behalf of humanity. The final cup he spoke of will not be offered nor drank from until the Bride enters her new home, the one provided for her, by her Groom.

Yeshua rose from the table, took off his outer clothing (his rabbinical robes), and wrapped a towel about his waist. He then poured water into a basin and began to wash his disciples' feet. Afterward, drying their feet with the towel wrapped around his waist, he welcomed his disciples into his family.

The washing of feet was a ritual of welcoming, which symbolized that a covenant relationship existed. The host offered rest as a welcoming gesture by removing travel dust from a guest's feet. Once the guest was welcomed, he was invited to abide under his host's roof as a family member. As a part of the host's household, the guest was then permitted to exercise the same authority as other household members. He could do so for as long as he remained under the covering of his host. This gifted authority meant the guest could speak and conduct business in the name of the host.

Yeshua, personally washing his disciples' feet, made such a commitment to them. John 15:7-8, *"If you abide in Me, and My words abide in you, you will ask what you desire, and it shall be done for you. By this, My Father is glorified, that you bear much fruit; so, you will be My disciples."*

Yeshua yearned for his disciples to understand they belonged to his Father. They were members of the Father's house, family members. He extended to them and those who would follow them the authority associated with his Father's house. Against their protest, *"Jesus answered, 'Unless I wash you, you have no part with me,'"* John 13:8.

When finished with the task at hand, Yeshua redressed. He put on his rabbinical garments, returned to his place at the table, and completed the meal with his co-inheritors.

Sometime later, when Yeshua and the inner circle of disciples were in Gethsemane (garden of the oil press), he entered a deep travail. Luke 22:41-44, *"He withdrew about a stone's throw beyond them, knelt down and prayed, 'Father, if you are willing, take this cup from me; yet not my will, but yours be done.' An angel from heaven appeared to him and strengthened him. And being in anguish, he prayed more earnestly, and his sweat was like drops of blood falling to the ground."*

Yeshua was about to receive a cup of bitterness, which contained the unrighteousness of previous and future generations. All sin had to be nailed to the cross. That indeed was a bitter cup for the Son of God!

The One who embodied eternal life was about to die a physical death. Think about that for a moment – the giver of life had to die! He had to submit to the spirit of Death so that his death might temporarily overtake his Life. That is mind-bending! Life had to be overcome by death so that Life-everlasting might be available to humanity!

To accomplish this was anguish. It was impossible without help. Yet Yeshua knew he had to complete the task of dying without his Father's help. And that meant he had to separate himself from his Father! How does God separate himself from himself? He would do so through faith – empowered by love.

Psalms 22:1, *"My God, my God, why have you forsaken me? Why are you so far from saving me, so far from the words of my groaning?"*

A brief time later, a detachment of soldiers and their commander and certain temple officials entered Gethsemane. They arrested Yeshua. After binding him, they took him, first to Annas, the father-in-law of Caiaphas, and then a brief time later, to Caiaphas himself.

Waiting for the soldiers and their prisoner with a few Sanhedrin members, Caiaphas called an illegal night court to assemble. In other words, he convened an ad hoc "kangaroo" court.

Surrounding him, his adversaries demanded to know if Yeshua had ever proclaimed himself to be the Messiah. Yeshua replied, "I have spoken openly to the world, always in synagogues or at the temple. In all the places where all Jews assembled. I have said nothing in total secret. Why do you question me? Ask those who heard me. Surely they know what I said."

One of those standing near struck Yeshua on the cheek, "Is this the way you answer the high priest?"

Yeshua responded, "If I said something wrong, testify as to what is wrong. But if I spoke the truth, why strike me?"

It was demanded of him, "Answer the question. What about the testimony that these men bring against you?"

Yeshua remained silent, giving no answer.

Using the authority of his office, the high priest ordered Yeshua to answer as a Jew, specifically as a rabbi. "I put you under oath, the oath of the Living God. Are you the expected Messiah, the Son of the Blessed One?"

Caiaphas cited Leviticus 5:1, *"If a person sins because he does not speak up when he hears a public charge to testify regarding something he has seen or learned about, he will be held responsible."*

Knowing full well that Yeshua was a rabbi. Thus, educated in all respects of the law, Caiaphas employed the Levitical rule to entrap Yeshua.

On the other hand, Yeshua, desiring to be without guilt, on any charge, replied saying, "What you say is true. I am. And you will see the Son of Man sitting at the right hand of the Mighty One and coming on the clouds of heaven."

Yeshua's answer frustrated Caiaphas. Provoked, he cried aloud, gripping the neck of his priestly robes with both hands, then forcefully he slung his arms outward in radical gesture. The collar of his robe ripped. Dramatically turning to the others present, Caiaphas screamed, "Why do we need any more witnesses? We have heard this blasphemy! What say you?"

A brief time later, the chief priests and the elders came to a decision. They determined Yeshua was guilty of blasphemy. And so, they had him bound that he might be led away and given over to Pilate. Their intent was to force Pilate to try Yeshua for treason against Rome in his civil court, which was also illegal because of Passover.

Not long afterward, when Yeshua stood before Pilate, the appointee of Rome queried, "Are you the king of the Jews?"

"It is as you say," Yeshua replied.

Quickly surmising why Yeshua was brought before him, Pilate announced he wanted nothing to do with the situation. Recognizing manipulation was at play, Pilate decided that any edict he issued concerning the matter would badly end his career. He told his soldiers to take the prisoner away.

The Roman soldiers took Yeshua into the Praetorium, where the attending officer called together the whole of his company. They were commanded to assemble that they might have sport with their prisoner.

Someone found a purple robe and wrapped it around Yeshua. Someone else twisted together a crown of thorns and set it upon his head, and as they did, they shouted, "Hail, king of the Jews!"

Again and again, they struck Yeshua on the head with a staff and spit upon him. Some even fell upon their knees, pretending to pay homage as they mocked the assertion that he was a king. Then, at last, they took him outside of the city in the third hour, and at that time, crucified him.

Once it was determined that they would crucify Yeshua of Nazareth, Pilate ordered a written notice of charge posted on the cross. He ordered that it be placed over Yeshua's head so all could read: THE KING OF JUDEA.

Those who passed by that horrible scene hurled insults at Yeshua, shaking their fists, they asserted loudly, "So! You were going to destroy the temple and build it again in three days. Come down from the cross and show us how you will do that. Save yourself if you are so powerful!"

At the sixth hour, unexplainable darkness fell over the city. Darkness covered the surrounding area till the ninth hour. That is until the moment that Yeshua cried out with a loud voice, *"Eloi, Eloi, lama sabachthani?"* Meaning - "My God, my God, why have you forsaken me?"

Using all his remaining physical strength, Yeshua breathed his last breath, and his spirit departed, leaving a beaten and bruised body behind on the cross.

When the centurion standing in front of Yeshua's cross heard his final cry and saw how he died, he said, "Surely this man was the Son of God!"

The Melchizedekian meaning of these things must not be overlooked. Thus, it is necessary to examine a few pertinent details. First, let's read Exodus 28:32: *"Make the robe of the ephod entirely of blue cloth, with an opening for the head in its center. There shall be a woven edge like a collar around this opening so that it will not tear."*

Next, Leviticus 10:6, "Uncover not your heads, neither rend your clothes."

Finally, Leviticus 21:10-11, *"The high priest, the one among his brothers who has had the anointing oil poured on his head and who has been ordained to wear the priestly* *garments, <u>must not let</u> his hair become unkempt or <u>rend his clothes</u>.*"

Caiaphas rent his robes; he disqualified himself from serving that Passover as a high priest. Remember, he grew angry and ripped his priestly robes when questioning Yeshua!

The verses from Leviticus clearly state that a high priest's robes must not be torn. Should they be the high priest is disqualified from duty. He may not stand before the altar nor officiate over any ceremony with torn garments.

As I wrote the previous sentence, I wondered if you asked: When questioning Yeshua, was Caiaphas wearing the robes of a high priest? The answer is – yes. Even though he was overseeing an illegal action, he did so as the high priest.

The time for Passover to begin was upon them. Both Caiaphas and his robes had been ceremonially cleansed. Likely, only a few hours before the trial took place.

According to Matthew 26: "*While he was still speaking, Judas, one of the twelve, arrived. With him was a large crowd armed with swords and clubs, sent from the chief priests and the elders of the people...At that time, Jesus said to the crowd, 'Am I leading a rebellion, that you have come out with swords and clubs to capture me? Every day I sat in the temple courts teaching, and you did not arrest me. But this has all taken place that the writings of the prophets might be fulfilled.' Then all the disciples deserted him and fled. Those who had arrested Jesus took him to <u>Caiaphas, the high priest</u>. Once he was there, the teachers of the law and the elders had assembled. But Peter followed him at a distance, right up to the <u>courtyard of the high priest</u>. He* *entered and sat down with the guards to see the outcome. The chief priests and the whole Sanhedrin were looking for false evidence against Jesus so that they could put him to death. But they did not find any, though many false witnesses came forward. Finally, two came forward and declared, 'This fellow said, "I am able to destroy the temple of God and rebuild it in three days."'*

Then the high priest stood up and said to Jesus, 'Are you not going to answer? What is this testimony that these men are bringing against you?' But Jesus remained silent.

The arrest of Yeshua and the subsequent questioning of him occurred in the wee hours of the morning. This indicates this trial was conducted illegally, against legal precedent.

Caiaphas was officiating as the Aaronic high priest. As high priest, he "said to him, 'I charge you under oath by the living God: Tell us if you are the Christ, the Son of God.'"

As previously noted, Caiaphas used Leviticus 5:1 to demand Yeshua answer or stand in violation of the law.

"Yes, it is as you say,' Jesus replied. 'But I say to all of you: In the future, you will see the Son of Man sitting at the right hand of the Mighty One and coming on the clouds of heaven.'

"Then the high priest tore his clothes and said, 'He has spoken blasphemy! Why do we need any more witnesses? Look, now you have heard the blasphemy. What do you think?'"

"He is worthy of death,' they answered."

There are several points to be made concerning Jesus' answer. First, the time of the Passover sacrifice neared. Close to where they stood in the temple court, priests were

79

preparing the temple's altar and the sacrificial offerings that would be made later for the Passover rituals. In truth, Yeshua, standing before Caiaphas, was preparing himself for sacrifice as the Melchizedek High Priest.

Caiaphas, the high priest of the Levitical Priesthood, faced Yeshua, the Melchizedek High Priest. Of course, Caiaphas believed himself the superior "priest," for he failed to recognize Yeshua's titles in any manner.

Regarding blood sacrifices, it also must be noted that only a high priest may officiate over any blood sacrifice that is offered to Yahweh. So, as these two high priests faced each other, a determination was being made: Which blood sacrifice would Yahweh receive? Both men would present to Yahweh later that same day, a blood sacrifice.

Blood was poured out on the temple's altar, while at the same time, blood was spilled just outside the city's gates – on a Cross.

Yeshua made "himself" the ultimate sacrifice. To guarantee his blood would be accepted, he would need to officiate over it. However, he would need to do so as a High Priest, the only acceptable High Priest from 'erets. Heaven had to view him as the "legal" representative of 'erets. In other words, Caiaphas had to be disqualified – found unacceptable as a high priest. If, for no other reason, that mock trial needed to happen so that Caiaphas would disqualify himself as high priest.

So, do you see the course of events? Lazarus died so Yeshua could resurrect him. Yeshua resurrected Lazarus to cause a reaction from the Lord of Sheol. The Lord of Sheol incited the Pharisees, and they illegally tried Yeshua.

Caiaphas demanded answers and grew angry at Truth when he responded.

All of these things happened so that the offerings placed on the temple's altars, which were prayed over by Caiaphas, would be deemed acceptable. Caiaphas disqualified himself. In so doing, he disqualified the Levitical Priesthood. Heaven's High Court would never again view Caiaphas or the Levitical priesthood as acceptable, as righteous.

Now, we need to dig deeper into the answer which angered Caiaphas, causing him to rip his robes. Jesus answered, "I say to all of you, In the future, you will see the <u>Son of Man</u> sitting at the right hand of the<u> Mighty One and coming on the clouds of heaven.</u>'"

Remember, Caiaphas had asked Yeshua if he claimed to be the "Son of God." Yeshua responded, "As you say; moreover, I put forth to you that I am also the Son of Man." Had Yeshua left his claim with merely being the "Son of God," chances are Caiaphas would have laughed. But when Yeshua said, "You gaze upon the Son of Man – he who sits at the right hand of power and appears with the 'clouds' of heaven," Caiaphas came apart.

To grasp the significance of what was said, we must be familiar with the writings of the Prophet Daniel. Daniel was the only Old Testament (*Tanakh*) writer to refer to the Messiah as the Son of Man.

Daniel depicted the Messiah as both a king and a high priest, which implied the term "Son of Man" belonged to Melchizedek. He described the Messiah as being ushered into the courts of heaven and the presence of the Ancient of Days where he would be seated as High Priest, at the Father's right hand.

Daniel 7:13-14, *"I saw in the night visions, and behold, one like the <u>Son of Man</u> came with the clouds of heaven and came to the Ancient of days, and they brought him near before him. And there was given him dominion, and glory, and a kingdom, that all people, nations, and languages, should serve him: his dominion is an everlasting dominion, which shall not pass away, and his kingdom that which shall not be destroyed."*

As a priest, Caiaphas was familiar with Daniel's scroll. He understood its prophetic implications. He was aware of all the meanings in its symbolic language. So, he knew what the rabbi who stood before him meant; the inference could not have been more exact. Yeshua was making a claim, as a rabbi unto the high priest – that he, Yeshua was Daniel's Son of Man, the King of *'Erets* – the High Priest of *'Erets.* Yeshua was testifying that he held the superior position by quoting Daniel 7:13.

Understanding Yeshua, Caiaphas, and the other Sanhedrin members realized that their livelihoods were being placed in jeopardy. Yeshua advised them that the system that provided them with power had just been shut down; that the days of their power were over.

These men, hearing Yeshua's words, grew afraid. Rather than accept him as the Son of God – they chose to kill him as the Son of Man.

"The former regulation is set aside because it was weak and useless, for the law made nothing perfect, and a better hope is introduced, by which we draw near to God. And it

was not without an oath! Others became priests without any oath, *but he became a priest with an oath when God said to him:* 'The Lord has sworn and will not change his mind: 'You are a priest forever.' *Because of this oath, Jesus has become the guarantee of a better covenant.* Now there have been many of those priests since death prevented them from continuing in office, but because Jesus lives forever, he has a permanent priesthood. Therefore, he is able to save completely those who come to God through him because he always lives to intercede for them. Such a high priest meets our need - one who is holy, blameless, pure, set apart from sinners, exalted above the heavens. Unlike the other high priests, he does not need to offer sacrifices day after day, first for his own sins and then for the sins of the people. He sacrificed for their sins once for all when he offered himself. For the law appoints as high priests men who are weak; but the oath, which came after the law, appointed the Son, who has been made perfect forever," Hebrews 7:18-28.

John 18:28-36, "*Then the Jews led Jesus from Caiaphas to the palace of the Roman governor. By now, it was early morning, and to avoid ceremonial uncleanness, the Jews did not enter the palace; they wanted to be able to eat the Passover. So, Pilate came out to them and asked, 'What charges are you bringing against this man?'*

'*If he were not a criminal,*' they replied, '*we would not have handed him over to you.*'

Pilate said, 'Take him yourselves and judge him by your own law.'

'*But we have no right to execute anyone,*' the Jews objected. This happened so that the words Jesus had spoken, *indicating the kind of death he was going to die, would be fulfilled.*

Pilate then went back inside the palace, summoned Jesus, and asked him, 'Are you the king of the Jews?'

'Is that your own idea,' Jesus asked, 'or did others talk to you about me?'

'Am I a Jew?' Pilate replied. 'It was your people and your chief priests who handed you over to me. What is it you have done?'

Jesus said, 'My kingdom is not of this world. If it were, my servants would fight to prevent my arrest by the Jews. But now my kingdom is from another place.'"

Note the phrase - *"My kingdom is not of this world."* Most translations use "world" because they see it as the equivalent of *"cosmos."* However, one of the meanings given by Strong's Lexicon defines *'cosmos'* as an orderly arrangement.

If we assume Yeshua was not referring to the world, meaning earth, but to an "order," – what order was he stating that his kingdom was of? The only viable answer: Melchizedek.

The phrase, *"my kingdom is from another place,"* is our confirmation. "Another place" is *enteuthen* (ent-yoo'-then). *Enteuthen* means to be "on both sides."

Please allow me to restate: "But hereafter, my kingdom is from both sides." Both sides of what? *The Cross!*

John 18:37- 19:30, *"You are a king, then!" said Pilate. Jesus answered, "You are right in saying I am a king. For this reason, I was born* (to be Melchizedek), *and for this, I came into the world to testify to the truth* (I have always been Melchizedek). *Everyone on the side of truth listens to me."*

"What is truth?" Pilate asked. With this, he went out again to the Jews and said, "I find no basis for a charge against him. But it is your custom for me to release to you one prisoner at the time of the Passover. Do you want me to release 'the king of the Jews?"

They shouted back, "No, not him! Give us Barabbas!"

(Barabbas had taken part in a rebellion, he was guilty of treason.)

Then Pilate took Jesus and had him flogged. The soldiers twisted together a crown of thorns and put it on his head.

The crown of thorns represented the twisting that came upon humanity in the Garden of Eden, which in theory, is the deception perpetrated by the adversary and the cause of Adam's sin.

Then, *"They clothed him in a purple* (purple denotes royalty) *robe and went up to him again and again, saying, "Hail, king of the Jews!"* ... It was the day of Preparation of Passover Week, about the sixth hour.

"Here is your king," Pilate said to the Jews.

But they shouted, "Take him away! Take him away! Crucify him!"

"Shall I crucify your king?" Pilate asked.

"We have no king but Caesar," the chief priests answered.

Finally, Pilate handed him over to them to be crucified.

So, the soldiers took charge of Jesus. Carrying his own cross, he went out to the place of the Skull (which in Aramaic is called Golgotha).

There they crucified him and two others, one on each side.

Pilate had a notice prepared and fastened to the cross. It read: JESUS OF NAZARETH, THE KING OF JUDEA.

The sign was written in Aramaic, Latin, and Greek, which meant many who passed by could read the placard seeing that the place where they crucified "criminals" was just outside the city.

The chief priests of the Jews protested to Pilate, "Do not write 'The King of the Jews,' but write he claimed to be king of the Jews."

Pilate answered, "What I have written, I have written."

When the soldiers crucified Jesus, they took his clothes, dividing them into four shares, one for each soldier, yet left his undergarment untouched. I need you to see why that was important.

Remember, Jesus was taken into custody after washing his disciples' feet. After he redressed and put back on his rabbinical robes. Consequently, when arrested in the garden, Jesus was wearing the same clothes. So he wore the standard rabbinical undergarment worn by priests. It was traditionally put on first; therefore, next to the body. And it was seamless, always made from one solid piece of material.

However, the outer garment of a high priest was blue. Which makes the robe handed to Yeshua by the soldiers in the Praetorium significant. It was blue and purple. Blue for the priesthood; purple for royalty.

At the foot of the Cross, the soldiers cast lots for his valuable white linen undergarment. *"Let's not rip it,"* they said to one another. *"Let's decide by lot who shall get it."*

Scripture was fulfilled. Yeshua's priestly robes remained untorn; they were protected by Holy Spirit, and Yeshua remained the cosmos' only qualified High Priest.

In the last moments, as he hung on the cross, Jesus said, *"I am thirsty."* A jar of wine vinegar was nearby. The soldiers soaked a sponge in the vinegar, then put the sponge on a hyssop stalk so that they could lift it to Jesus' lips. When he had received the drink, Jesus said, *"It is finished."* With that, he bowed his head and gave up his spirit.

Yeshua had fought to breathe as long as he could. As the High Priest, he alone could decree the blood sacrifice as complete; consumed. When he could no longer sustain life without help, he asserted loudly, *"It is FINISHED!"*

The significance of his words? They are the benedictory words of a High Priest, which he loudly proclaims before walking away from the altar's consumed sacrifice!

All sin: past, present, and future was marked paid with that proclamation! Even so, his assignment as the High Priest of the order belonging to Melchizedek had just begun.

Romans 6:9-11, *"…knowing that Christ, having been raised from the dead, dies no more. Death no longer has dominion over Him. For the death that He died, He died to sin once for all; but the life that He lives, He lives to God. Likewise, you also reckon yourselves to be dead indeed to sin, but alive to God in Christ Jesus our Lord."*

1 Corinthians 15:20-22, *"But now Christ is risen from the dead, and has become the firstfruits of those who have fallen asleep. For since by man came death, by Man also came the resurrection of the dead. For as in Adam all die, even so in Christ, all shall be made alive."*

After his death, Yeshua preached the message of the Melchizedek Kingdom to those in *Sheol.* Three days later, he awoke from the "dead"- He became the Firstfruits of the Great Resurrection.

John 20:1-17, *"Early on the first day of the week, while it was still dark, Mary Magdalene went to the tomb and saw that the stone had been removed from the entrance. So, she came running to Simon Peter and the other disciple, the one Jesus loved, and said, 'They have taken the Lord out of the tomb, and we don't know where they have put him!"*

Peter and the other disciple started for the tomb. Both were running, but the other disciple outran Peter and reached the tomb first. He bent over and looked in at the strips of linen lying there but did not go in. Then Simon Peter, who was behind him, arrived and went into the tomb. He saw the strips of linen lying there, as well as the burial cloth that had been around Jesus' head. The cloth was folded up by itself, separate from the linen. Finally, the other disciple, who had reached the tomb first, also went inside. He saw and believed. They still did not understand from Scripture that Jesus had to rise from the dead. Then the disciples went back to their homes, but Mary stood outside the tomb crying. As she wept, she bent over to look into the tomb and saw two angels in white, seated where Jesus' body had been, one at the head and the other at the foot.

They asked her, "Woman, why are you crying?"

"They have taken my Lord away," she said, "and I don't know where they have put him." At this, she turned around and saw Jesus standing there, but she did not realize that it was Jesus.

INTRODUCING MELCHIZEDEK AND HIS KINGDOM

"Woman," he said, "why are you crying? Who is it you are looking for?"

Thinking he was the gardener, she said, "Sir, if you have carried him away, tell me where you have put him, and I will get him."

Jesus said to her, "Mary."

She turned toward him and cried out in Aramaic, "Rabboni!" (which means Teacher).

Jesus said, "Do not touch me, for I have not yet returned to the Father. Go instead to my brothers and tell them, 'I am returning to my Father and your Father, to my God and your God.'"

When Yeshua left the tomb, he left his burial clothes behind. Along with that fact, there is a question that must be asked: What did he wear? From where did he obtain a garment? The Roman soldiers had taken his garments; he had hung on the cross naked. When preparing his body for burial, the disciples adhered to the custom of their day. They wrapped strips of linen about his head and covered his naked body with a shroud. Yet, when Yeshua left the tomb, he left the burial shroud behind.

The most plausible answer concerning this perplexity is that the angels supplied him with the vesture of a High Priest. If that be so, then that explains why Mary Magdalene was admonished not to touch him. She was not to taint his sanctified attire. That of a High Priest.

After leaving Mary, Yeshua ascended into heaven. There, placed his blood upon the altar of Yahweh's Holy Temple, doing so officially as Melchizedek, as the eternal High Priest.

Daniel 7:13, *"behold, one like the Son of man came with the clouds of heaven and came to the Ancient of days, and they brought him near before him."*

Ephesians 1:19-23, *"And what is the exceeding greatness of his power to us who believe, according to the working of his mighty power, which he wrought in Christ, when he raised him from the dead, and set him at his own right hand in the heavenly places, far above all principality, and power, and might, and dominion, and every name that is named, not only in this world but also in that which is to come: and hath put all things under his feet and gave him to be the head over all things to the church, which is his body, the fullness of him that fills all."*

Chapter 5 - The Rebellion

Why do the nations conspire, and the peoples plot in vain? The kings of the earth take their stand, and the rulers gather against the LORD (Yahweh) and against his Anointed One (the Messiah). 'Let us break their chains,' they say, 'and throw off their fetters.' The One enthroned in heaven laughs; the Lord (Yahweh) scoffs at them. Then He rebukes them in His anger and terrifies them in His wrath, saying, 'I have installed my King (Melek) on Zion (the capital of God's earthly government), my holy hill.'

"I will proclaim the decree of the LORD: He said to me, 'You are my Son; today I have become your Father. Ask of me, and I will make the nations your inheritance, the ends of the earth your possession. You will rule them with an iron scepter; you will dash them to pieces like pottery.' Therefore, you kings, be wise; be warned, you rulers of the earth. Serve the LORD with fear and rejoice with trembling. Kiss the Son, lest he be angry, and you be destroyed in your way, for his wrath can flare up in a moment. Blessed are all who take refuge in him." Psalms 2

Hebrews 2:1, *"We must pay more careful attention, therefore, to what we have heard, so that we do not drift away."* This verse advises the reader to pay close attention to the gospel "first preached." Specifically, what was the gospel first preached? It was the good news that Melchizedek and his kingdom were restored; thus, 'erets was again under his reign!

Hebrews continued to caution that if the church failed to preach this kingdom message, the same web of deception, which occurred before Yeshua's coming, would again appear. To emphasize his point as to which message was superior, the one delivered by angels or the one taught by the apostles of Yeshua, the author of Hebrews stated the following: *"For if the word spoken through angels proved steadfast, and every transgression and disobedience received a just reward, how shall we escape if we neglect so great a salvation, which was at first spoken by the Lord and confirmed to us by those who heard Him?"*

Galatians 3:19, *"What purpose then does the law serve? It was added because of transgressions, till the Seed should come to whom the promise was made, and it was appointed through angels by the hand of a mediator."*

Spirit entities from the unseen realm have intentionally injected themselves into human affairs since the Garden of Eden. Some for the benefit of mankind, others for the harm. The Old Testament leaves little doubt on that score. For instance, in Deuteronomy 33:2, *"And he* (Moses) *said, 'Jehovah came from Sinai, and rose from Seir unto them. He shined forth from mount Paran. He came from* (or with) *the ten thousand holy ones: At his right hand was a fiery law...."* This entourage accompanying Yahweh was *qodesh* (holy). *Qodesh* refers to the dedication or the holiness of a person or place.

Paul understood Deuteronomy 33:2 referenced "angels" and not humans. "Angels" is placed in quotes because Paul wrote *aggelos*. *Aggelos* means messengers.

Still, *aggelos* was not a word commonly applied to human messengers. But was used when referring to spirit messengers, especially those sent by God. That is why Paul emphasized that the "law" was "appointed through *aggelos.*" In other words, they delivered the law to Moses because they assisted Moses as commanded by Yahweh.

"Torah" infers revelation yet is most often translated as law. The *Torah* (the five scrolls of Moses) was written as a teaching device; to instruct the people concerning Yahweh's will, primarily in the establishment of Yahweh's Kingdom in the Promised Land. Implementing this "law of Moses" is what the "angels" supervised.

If we believe the Bible, we know angels exist and interact with humanity. So, how have they influenced human society? The answer depends upon whether the angels we speak of are *qodesh* or not.

Not all angels or angelic. The word angel was derived from *'angelos* [Greek]. The Hebrew word is *mal'akh*. Both translates as "messenger," one sent to deliver a communique. Additionally, both terms are gender nonspecific.

The English word angel is also non-specific and an over-used term often applied to every created being from the unseen realms. The reality is not all beings from the unseen spirit world are identical. They are many and are varied. They have a society, ranking, and government. Some govern, and others are governed. Their civilization has both the holy (*qodesh*) and the evil (rebellious).

That is why the Creator placed a boundary between "his" domain and the rebels. Their realm is the underworld, and God placed 'erets between the holy and the unholy as a "field" of decision.

Heaven is God's; therefore, it is holy (*qodesh*). *Qodesh* means "set apart for God's use." On the other hand, the underworld is evil and profane, therefore, assigned to the rebellious – the ones who defy Yahweh.

"How you are fallen from heaven,
O Lucifer, son of the morning!
How you are cut down to the ground,
You who weakened the nations!
For you have said in your heart:
'I will ascend into heaven,
I will exalt my throne above the stars of God.
I will also sit on the mount of the congregation,
On the farthest sides of the north.
I will ascend above the heights of the clouds,
I will be like the Most High.'
Yet you shall be brought down to Sheol,
To the lowest depths of the Pit." Isaiah 14:12-15 NKJV

Lucifer is a Latin word meaning "the one who carries light." The transliterated Hebrew presents this phrase as *heylel ben shachar.* Which translates as "the morning star, which is derived from light."

Ezekiel 28:12-19, "*Thus, says Yahweh, 'You were the seal of perfection, full of wisdom and perfect in beauty. You were in Eden, the garden of God; every precious stone was your* *covering: The sardius, topaz, and diamond, beryl, onyx, and jasper, sapphire, turquoise, and emerald with gold. The workmanship of your timbrels and pipes was prepared for you on the day you were created. You were the <u>anointed cherub who covers;</u> I established you; you were on the holy mountain of God; you walked back and forth in the midst of fiery stones. You were perfect in your ways from the day you were created till iniquity was found in you. By the abundance of your trading, you became filled with violence within, and you sinned. Therefore, I cast you as a profane thing out of the mountain of God; And I destroyed you, O covering cherub, from the midst of the fiery stones. Your heart was lifted up because of your beauty; you corrupted your wisdom for the sake of your splendor; I cast you to the ground, I laid you before kings, that they might gaze at you. You defiled your sanctuaries by the multitude of your iniquities by the iniquity of your trading; Therefore, I brought fire from your midst; it devoured you, and I turned you to ashes upon the earth in the sight of all who saw you. All who knew you among the peoples are astonished at you; you have become a horror and shall be no more forever.'"*

Ezekiel's discourse describes a cherished entity who walked with great authority as a throne guardian. But then he was cast down from his high-ranking position because he fell from grace. Chiefly, because he led an uprising against Yahweh. He defiled himself and corrupted all who he persuaded to join his rebellion.

"And you say, 'I am a god, I sit in the seat of gods (elohim)...,'" Ezekiel 28:2. The implication of this portion of Ezekiel's narrative is that this cherub was a member of

Yahweh's Divine Council. And that initially, he served Yahweh with distinction, "*you were perfect in your ways from the day you were created, till iniquity was found in you.*"

Now that we clearly understand that spirit beings can be holy or unholy let's glance back to the beginning of this chapter. Psalm 2 asks, "Why do the *goyim – ragash?*" The *goy*(im) are people (nations) who live outside the covenants of Yahweh (outside the Kingdom of God). *Ragash* means to conspire. Though, the more profound meaning conveys tumult. According to the dictionary, tumult is a violent and noisy commotion, chaos, disorder, and agitation that causes confusion.

"*Why do the people plot in vain?*" These words in transliterated Hebrew: *leom hagah riyq*? *Leom* means community; *hagah*, a roaring sound created from anger; *riyq* refers to something worthless or empty, which has no purpose.

Hence the question could be translated as: "Why do those who live outside of covenant stir up confusion and the community roar with anger from something that has no purpose?"

Psalms 2:2 continues, "*The kings of the earth ['erets] station themselves against Yahweh and against <u>his</u> Messiah.*"

Messiah refers to the king/priest anointing.

So, I'm stating that Psalms 2 is a picture portraying a supreme ruler strategizing against Yahweh and his anointed Melchizedek. He brings together a group of like-minded beings to plot against the Godhead. In other words, the "authorities and powers, who are world-rulers of this dark night and are the spirits of evil in the heavens," said one to another, "let's break out of our chains and throw off our fetters." These unholy actors decided to "do away with the curse" Yahweh pronounced upon them and cast down Yahweh's government.

The curse they sought to destroy is the curse of death. Death, in this case, refers to the final destiny of all who revolt against the sovereignty of the Creator.

The point? Celestials (spirit beings) can die. That is if they rebelled against Yahweh. Disregard the fact that they are spirits. They shall die the "second death."

1 Corinthians 15:39-40, "*All flesh is not the same flesh, but there is one kind of flesh of men, another flesh of animals, another of fish, and another of birds. There are also celestial bodies and terrestrial bodies, but the <u>glory</u> of the celestial is one, and the <u>glory</u> of the terrestrial is another.*" As used in this passage, glory means honor or dignity, relating to station or rank.

Paul was not writing exclusively about immortality. He was teaching on corruption and the great resurrection. He pointed out that the "second death" will not affect those resurrected with honor.

Revelation 2:11, "*He who has an ear, let him hear what the Spirit says to the churches. He who overcomes shall not be hurt by the <u>second death</u> -*" (thanatou tou deutero "death the second"). This second death is an everlasting separation – forever and ever - apart from Yahweh, the source of life.

Typically, death occurs when a human body ceases to breathe or its brain fails to sustain life. Indeed, there is truth in those assertions. Yet, according to the Bible, when accurately viewed, permanent (everlasting) death is not a physical event but a spiritual one.

2 Corinthians 5:8, *"We are of good courage, and we would be away from the body and be home with the Lord."* Paul was stressing the absence of a body should not be viewed as death. Essentially, Paul distinguished between the soul (spirit) and body.

All created beings are everlasting – Yahweh, being the Father of all. Zechariah 12:1, *"Thus says the Lord, who stretches out the heavens, lays the foundation of the earth and forms the spirit of man within him...."*

Thus, we should view the flesh as a covering—a garment worn by a spirit. The garment material covering celestials is different from the material used to form terrestrials. Terrestrial flesh is mortal, whereas celestials are immortal.

I've gone around the proverbial mountain to expose this truth: Terrestrial beings, as well as celestials, are primarily spiritual in nature. The Creator intended for all to be immortal – to dwell with the Creator forever and ever.

The word spirit was derived from the Latin *spiritus*. *Spiritus* simply refers to the breath in the body. However, if we genuinely comprehend the concept, spirit refers to the soul's life energy.

Once formed, the soul never loses its life source, its energy. It continues to exist. This is true, regardless of the fabric that covers the soul.

Is there more than one source of life? Of course not! God is the Creator. He alone is the source of all life-giving energy.

2 Corinthians 4:16, *"Therefore, we do not lose heart. Even though our outward man is perishing, yet the inward man is being renewed day by day."*

Spirits are renewed through interaction with God. All spirits are renewed in the same manner. If that is the case, then being separated from Yahweh is death.

I believe that the bodies of celestials are formed by light particles, and that is why Paul wrote in 2 Corinthians 11:14, *"And no wonder, for Satan himself, masquerades as an angel of light."*

James 1:17 refers to the Creator as the Father of Lights, so I made a connection: Light creates life!

Returning to this chapter's subject, the rebellion of Psalms 2, the chains the rebels sought to break are the same ones Jude wrote about. *"And the angels who did not keep their proper domain, but left their own abode, He has reserved in everlasting chains under darkness for the judgment of the great day...."*

As I began my research for this chapter, I asked myself, how dark can matter be? I discovered a dark exists that absorbs photons at the subatomic level. Wow! Could that be the description of outer darkness?

To be consumed atom by atom in an everlasting existence would indeed be a reason to gnash one's teeth. It would be a place of intense, fiery pain. However, knowing that you are without hope is the greater agony. For you see, the second death is dying continually – it will go on and on, forever and ever.

Psalms 2:4 shifts the reader's attention to the courts of heaven, where he is permitted to see an enthroned Yahweh laughing. God is not laughing at anyone's agony but because his Anointed King shall rule forever and ever.

Yahweh 'aph – which means he snorted. He blew his breath through his nose. Then opened his mouth to release a burning, fiery stream of harsh words, which terrified the rebellious. Yahweh's words were so intense; so powerful when they hit their mark, the rebellious rulers quaked.

Yahweh said: "I have (past tense) installed my King on Zion, my Holy Hill." In other words, he prophesied his intent, which pointed to the Cross.

Yahweh was pointing, finger in the air, to the place of exchange. The place where the eternal Melchizedek would take possession of his throne and reign forever. (Remember the Messiah cried out as High Priest from the Cross, "it is finished!")

According to 2 Samuel 5:7, Zion was a "stronghold...the same.... the city of David." Zion, or Tsiyown in Hebrew, refers to the place of righteousness. That is why the Melchizedek governs from Zion.

Zion is "his" city; "his" mountain. Literally and figuratively, Zion is analogous to the Garden of Eden. This means it is possible to track Zion, throughout Scripture, as the seat of 'erets government. Going from the Garden of Eden to David's palace and New Jerusalem.

But note, David wasn't anointed in Zion. Samuel anointed David at Bethlehem. So, Psalms 2 wasn't referring to David as the king to be installed on the Holy Hill.

The transliterated Hebrew, nacak, means installed. However, in that same word is a greater significance that we mustn't overlook. In effect, Yahweh stated a libation of oil was upon 'his' King. That anointing was so substantial it enabled the King to fulfill all that was assigned to him. And that all-encompassing anointing is the reason Yeshua was the Messiah – the Anointed One!

Yahweh continued to clarify by speaking directly to the Messiah-King, *"You are my Son; today I have begotten you..."*

Yahweh has only one begotten Son. Begotten is *yalad*. It means to show lineage. The lineage of Yeshua was not just declared in the Gospels. It was announced long before Yeshua appeared in the flesh. As a matter of fact, Yahweh decreed Yeshua's genealogy in Psalms 2:7.

Turning to his Son, Yahweh began prophesying: *"Ask of me,* (demand of me) *and I will make (*add, ascribe, appoint*) the nations* (the *goyim* as) *your inheritance* (your possession) *... the ends of* (by the end of the age) *the earth* (shall be) *in your possession."*

Psalms 2 decreed a far-reaching prophecy. Yeshua would lay hold of 'erets by seizing it from the adversary's hands. *"You will rule them* (the inhabitants of 'erets) *with an iron* (firm) *scepter* (authority)*; you will dash them (the rebellious) to pieces like pottery."*

Dash could be translated as to scatter. The inference: Yeshua would rule the enemy's strongholds, scattering the dust of their army as broken pottery, spreading them as nothingness.

Daniel 2: 44-45, *"And in the days of these kings shall the God of heaven set up a kingdom, which shall never be destroyed: and the kingdom shall not be left to other people, but it shall break in pieces and consume all these kingdoms, and it shall stand forever. Forasmuch as you saw that the stone was cut out of the mountain without hands and that it broke in pieces the iron, the brass, the clay, the silver, and the gold; the great God hath made known to the king what shall come to pass hereafter...."*

Most royal scepters are made of gold. However, in Psalms 2, Yeshua was given a rod of iron. Biblical imagery suggests iron represents celestial power. Therefore, Yeshua was given cosmic authority so that he might crush all opposition – no matter whether it was of the seen or unseen realm. Thus, when portrayed as holding the iron scepter, Yeshua is the Lion of Judah, the warring King.

Psalms 2 concludes with a warning: *"Therefore, you kings be wise; be warned, you rulers of the earth* (you who speak over the government of 'erets). *Serve* (enslave yourself) *to the LORD* (Yahweh) *with fear* (with dread because of his authority) *and rejoice* (make yourself joyful) *with trembling. Kiss* (arm and align yourself with) *the Son, lest He be angry* (and breathe hard upon you) *and you* (too) *be destroyed in your* way (because your rebellion has failed)*; for His* (Yahweh's) *wrath can flare up in a moment* (the least provocation activates him. He is zealous. And demands respect be given to the Son)*. Blessed are all who take refuge in Him* (for they are the ones who have hope of life everlasting)."

When he came to 'erets as a babe, Yeshua's ranking was lesser than the ordering of angels, only because he came as a human child, to parents that were not assigned to rule. Yet while he was in 'erets, he became Melchizedek.

Yeshua overcame the rebellious – because he learned obedience. He came to the realm of 'erets with lesser power than that given to angels, but nonetheless, forever, he shall have the greater authority. After his ascension, ALL honor, authority, and power became his, not only within 'erets but throughout the cosmos. Owing to his perfection gained through obedience, the Son of Man was given the seat next to the Father.

Seated at the Father's right hand, Yeshua is ever living to represent humanity. He desires to help all who will believe in him.

Yeshua tasted the death of separation from the Source of Light so that no human, who believes in him, need ever be subjugated to the curse of the second death. He did not taste death to remove its curse so that the angels might become his inheritance. Meaning they are not co-inheritors.

The book of Hebrews states these things in this manner: The message we must preach "*was confirmed* <u>to us by those who heard him</u>" (Yeshua's disciples). *God* (the Father) *also testified to it by signs, wonders, various miracles, and gifts of the Holy Spirit distributed according to his will. It is not to angels that he has subjected the world to come about which we are speaking. But there is a place where someone has testified:* (Psalms 8) *'What is* a (mortal) *man that you are mindful of him* (that You mark him), *the son of man* (as the son of Adam) *that you care for him? You made him a little lower* (he was brought forth with less power) *than the angels; you crowned* (encircled) *him with glory* (deity) *and honor* (majesty) *and put*

103

everything under his feet.'" (The idiom 'under his feet' means whatever is under his foot – is in his possession.)

"In putting everything under Him, God (Yahweh) left nothing that is not subject to Him (Yeshua now possesses the territory stolen by the adversary). Yet, at present, we do not see everything subject to Him. (In other words, we do not as yet discern that mankind has the right to rule) but we see (we can discern) Jesus, who was (also) made a little lower than the angels, (Yeshua, while in the realm of *'erets,* exhibited no power of his own, but is) now crowned with glory and honor because He suffered death, so that by the grace of God (Yeshua came in the authority of Yahweh). He tasted death for everyone; in bringing many sons to glory, it was fitting that God, for whom and through whom everything exists, should make the author of their salvation perfected (Yeshua completed all assignments) through suffering (the affliction that removed the curse of death). Both the one (Yeshua) who makes men holy (righteous) and those who are made holy (righteous) are of the same family. So, Jesus is not ashamed to call them brothers. He says, 'I will declare your name to my brothers; in the presence of the congregation, I will sing your praises.' And again, 'I will put my trust in him.' And again, He says, 'Here am I, and the children God has given me.'"

Chapter 6 - The Kingdom

Matthew 4:17, "From that time Jesus began to preach and to say, "Repent, <u>for the kingdom of heaven</u> is at hand."

Matthew 6:9-13, "This, then, is how you should pray: 'Our Father in heaven, hallowed be your name, your kingdom come, your will be done on earth as it is in heaven. Give us today our daily bread. Forgive us our debts, as we also have forgiven our debtors. And lead us not into temptation but deliver us from the evil one.'"

Matthew 6:33-34, "But seek first the kingdom of God and His righteousness, and all these things shall be added to you.

Only the Gospel of Matthew uses the phrase "kingdom of heaven." Which we can discover by examining Strong's Concordance, is *basileía tœin ouranœin,* in Greek.

Typically, *basileia* is translated as "kingdom." And, of course, the structure of government ruled by a king is a kingdom.

Matthew recorded that Yeshua instructed the people to seek the kingdom of God and righteousness. In other words, the Kingdom of Righteousness, the domain Yeshua oversees as the King of Righteousness!

Ouranos, translated as "heaven," carries several implications, all of which make the use of this word in relationship to government interesting. In certain instances, *ouranos* is translated as the sky. Still, by implication, *ouranos* often referred to the upper regions of the cosmos. Whenever *ouranos* was used in connection with Yahweh, it referred to the place of his eternal abode.

John the Baptist came preaching Matthew 3:2, *"… Repent for the kingdom of heaven is at hand."*

"Repent" - *metanoeo* means to think differently.

Eggizo - "at hand" means to draw near; to be nigh unto; to approach.

Matthew 3:2 paraphrased: Think differently – the kingdom of heaven is approaching 'erets.

Throughout this writing, I have used the word 'erets rather than earth for the simple reason 'erets is a realm, not a planet. The ancients viewed life as existing in three territorial domains, heaven, 'erets, and the underworld. When these three were considered collectively, they were viewed as the entirety of the cosmos.

In that regard, the ancients believed the underworld belonged to 'erets; it was "under" the order of 'erets. Thus, in the strictest biblical sense, the only "legal" realms of existence – heaven and 'erets. That point of view explains why Genesis 1:1 reads: *"In the beginning, God created the heaven and 'erets."*

Heavens or *Shamayim* belongs to Yahweh; it is under the "order" of Yahweh. *'Erets* belongs to Melchizedek. The underworld, or *Sheol*, is also Melchizedek's. He holds the keys. Revelation 1:18, *"I am He who lives, and was dead, and behold, I am alive forevermore. Amen. And I have the keys of Hades and of Death."*

However, that doesn't explain the Kingdom of the Melchizedek in strict terms. So, let's dig deeper.

Romans 14:17, "For the kingdom of God is not meat and drink; but righteousness, and peace, and joy in the Holy Spirit."

Hebrews 11:6, *"But without faith, it is impossible to please Him, for he who comes to God must believe that He is and that He is a rewarder of those who diligently seek Him."*

2 Corinthians 5:7, *"We live by faith.*

Terms such as righteousness, peace, joy, and faith are sometimes elusive. Often these terms are thought of as emotions. The reality is they are "states" of existence – more specifically, they are mindsets. Another view would be to see them as determinations.

To abide in a state (mindset) of peace means we are "faithing." Faith creates peace and joy. That is why faith is an "evidential" substance, accomplishing that which we could not "see" when we first believed.

Abraham is a perfect example of how this principle works. When he was first called out of the "world" and instructed to go to the city of God, he went to Melchizedek Shem.

Hebrews 11:8-10, *"By faith, Abraham obeyed when he was called to go out to the place which he would receive as an inheritance. And he went out, not knowing where he was going. By faith, he dwelt in the land of promise as in a foreign country, dwelling in tents with Isaac and Jacob, the heirs with him of the same promise; for he waited for the city which has foundations, whose builder and maker is God."*

Abram never saw the "city" of God, nor did he have an heir when he received the promise that he would be a father

107

of many. But yet, he believed. The fact that he did is what gained him an heir.

Abraham's faith was counted unto him for righteousness. His belief in the promises made to him propelled him into the Melchizedek Kingdom. Consequently, he had a son who became a Melchizedek.

"He answered and said unto them because it is given unto you to know the mysteries of the kingdom of heaven, *but to them, it is not given. For whosoever hath, to him shall be given, and he shall have more abundance: but whosoever has not* (understood the mysteries), *from him shall be taken away even that which he has. Therefore, speak I to them in parables: because they see not; and hearing they hear not, neither do they understand,"* Matthew 13:11-23.

Hebrews 11 lists a few of those who received miracles through faith - Abel, Enoch, Noah, Abraham, and Sarah. Others, as well, for the list continues as evidence of Yahweh's faithfulness to those who believe. All received promises because they were obedient; they were faithful.

In some manner, each of the above had faith in the Kingdom. They accepted the government established by God. Hence, they were "kingdom" minded.

Another great mystery of the kingdom is using authority properly. This trait was exemplified by Yeshua. He spoke with confidence because he understood Yahweh's sovereignty.

Although Yeshua is a member of the Godhead, he did not come in his own authority. He came to "earn" authority by receiving it from Yahweh - through obedience.

Yeshua placed his faith in Yahweh's ability to fulfill all promises made to him. Psalms 2 recorded the commitment to install him as King, as the eternal Melchizedek. Believing in these promises, Yeshua proclaimed himself as the Melchizedek. He did so, even though all other evidence was against him.

Yeshua promised his disciples that they could tap into Yahweh's authority, precisely as he had if they believed (walked in faith).

Matthew 16:19, *"And I will give unto you the keys of the kingdom of heaven, and whatsoever you bind on earth shall be bound in heaven: and whatsoever you loose on earth shall be loosed in heaven."*

Keys lock (bind) gates or open (loosen) them. It could be rightfully said that the keys of the kingdom establish the law of the kingdom. So, to paraphrase Yeshua: Whatever is legal in the realm of heaven is lawful in the domain of 'erets. Conversely, whatsoever is unlawful in heaven is illegal in 'erets.

Does God have a government other than the Melchizedek system? No! So, the Kingdom of Heaven is the Kingdom of God – the Melchizedek Kingdom.

Yeshua preached his first kingdom message after returning from the wilderness and his forty-day fast.

He proclaimed: *"Blessed are the poor in spirit: for theirs is the kingdom of heaven."*

In other words, "Blessed are those who are needy in their spiritual life. They are the ones who shall inherit the kingdom.

"Blessed are they which do hunger and thirst after righteousness: for they shall be filled."

Yeshua's sermon also introduced "royal law." He basically said, "If you seek the Lord, your God, with all your heart and love your neighbor as yourself, then you can reach out and lay hold of the kingdom of heaven." So, the royal law simply stated is love God, love your neighbor.

Matthew 5:20, *"For I say unto you, that except your righteousness shall exceed the righteousness of the scribes and Pharisees, you shall in no case enter into the kingdom of heaven."*

The Scribes translated the Levitical law into the various languages of their day. The Pharisees were a sect of rabbis who argued for a strict interpretation of the Levitical law. Both groups were considered qualified to practice law. Accordingly, their righteousness was in the "letter" – not the "spirit" of the law they revered.

However, the heart of Yeshua's message was that the kingdom of heaven may be obtained only by faith – faith in whom? In what? In HIM – that he was who he said he was – the Melchizedek appointed by Yahweh. That he was the inheritor of the "KINGDOM!"

Matthew 7:21-27, *"Not everyone that says unto me, Lord, Lord, shall enter into the kingdom of heaven; but he that does the will of my Father which is in heaven. Many will say to me in that day, 'Lord, Lord, have we not prophesied in your name? and in thy name have cast out devils? and in thy name done many wonderful works?' And then will I profess unto them, 'I never knew you: depart from me you workers of iniquity.' Therefore, whosoever hears these sayings of* *mine and does them, I will liken him unto a wise man, which built his house upon a rock, and the rain descended, and the floods came, and the winds blew, and beat upon that house. It fell not, <u>for it was founded upon a rock</u>. And every one that hears these sayings of mine, and doeth them not, shall be likened unto a foolish man, which built his house upon the sand: and the rain descended, and the floods came, and the winds blew, and beat upon that house; and it fell, and great was the fall of it."*

Yeshua told the people to build upon a "rock." He would have used the word "*eben*." *Eben* translates as "rock" - a natural stone that has not been fashioned in any manner. *Eben* is spelled אבן (*aleph-bet-nun*) and pictographically nba portrays the "seed of the house of the strong leader."

Yeshua is that Seed, the Son of Yahweh. Accordingly, the Melchizedek – the King of Righteousness. He told his audience to build their faith in him, who he is, and then walk in his authority.

Matthew 8:8-13, *"The centurion answered and said, 'Lord, I am not worthy that you should come under my roof: but speak the word only, and my servant shall be healed. <u>For I am a man under authority</u>, having soldiers under me: <u>and I say</u> to this man, 'Go,' and he goes; and to another, 'Come,' and he comes; and to my servant, 'Do this,' and he does it.'*

"When Jesus heard it, he marveled and said to them that followed, 'Verily I say unto you, I have not found so great faith, no, not in Israel. And I say unto you, that many shall come from the east and west and shall sit down with Abraham, and Isaac, and Jacob, in <u>the kingdom of heaven</u>. But the children of the kingdom shall be cast out into outer

darkness: there shall be weeping and gnashing of teeth.' And Jesus said unto the centurion, 'Go thy way; and as you have believed, so be it done for you.' His servant was healed in the selfsame hour."

A commander must command, which is another way of saying that a king does not need to physically encounter everyone in his kingdom to enforce his law. The centurion understood this principle and the proper manner of exercising power. He recognized Yeshua knew how to do the same.

Yeshua is "the" Melchizedek. As believers in him, we must have faith that his words shall be enforced when we speak.

His words are like "keys" – they either lock or unlock the kingdom – across and throughout the cosmos.

Seeing with our eyes or hearing with our ears does not prove the truth. Evidence comes from knowing Truth – knowing HIM.

The centurion had obviously seen or heard that Yeshua had performed miracles, but that wasn't what motivated him; it was the weight of authority with which Yeshua spoke. *"For I myself am a man under authority,"* Matthew 8:9.

Due to his understanding of authority, the centurion had faith in the Messiah's word. His faith was translated into righteousness. In turn, his righteousness placed him in the Kingdom of the Melchizedek.

The moment he believed the centurion obtained right standing with Melchizedek. His faith demanded justice. Perceiving Yeshua's authority was absolute, the centurion believed what he was requesting for his servant would be accomplished.

The foundations of God's throne are righteousness and justice. Justice is an equitable measurement that makes right that which was formerly wrong. The centurion came to Yeshua, seeking a decree. It never entered his mind to ask Yeshua to personally administer the order, only to speak it. My point: the centurion viewed Yeshua as having ultimate authority – the authority of a king, never mind that he wasn't familiar with the Melchizedek system or its laws. Regardless, he believed in its authority.

Matthew 16:13-19 *"When Jesus came into the coasts of Caesarea Philippi, he asked his disciples, 'Who do men say that I, the Son of man am?' And they said, 'Some say that you are John the Baptist; some, Elias; and others, Jeremias, or one of the prophets.' He said unto them, 'But whom do you say that I am?' And Simon Peter answered, 'You are the Messiah, the Son of the living God.'*

"And Jesus answered and said unto him, 'Blessed are you, Simon Barjona. Flesh and blood did not reveal this unto you; but my Father which is in heaven. And I say also that you are Peter, (a piece of the rock) *and upon this rock* (Yeshua) *I will build my church, and the gates of hell shall not prevail against it. And I will give unto you the keys to the kingdom of heaven: and whatsoever you shall bind on earth shall be bound in heaven: and whatsoever you shalt loose on earth shall be loosed in heaven."*

Yeshua's keys, which he gave to Peter and the others, were promises. He shall build his "church" – it shall withstand the gates of Hades!

Ephesians 1:3-10 *"Praise be to the God and Father of our Lord Jesus Christ, who has blessed us in the heavenly realms with every spiritual blessing in Christ. For he chose us in him before the creation of the world to be holy and blameless in his sight. In love, he predestined us to be adopted as his sons through Jesus Christ, in accordance with his pleasure and will to the praise of his glorious grace, which he has freely given us in the One he loves. In him, we have redemption through his blood, the forgiveness of sins, in accordance with the riches of God's grace that he lavished on us with all wisdom and understanding. And he made known to us the mystery of his will according to his good pleasure, which he purposed in Christ, to be put into effect when the times will have reached their fulfillment to bring all things in heaven and on earth together under one head, even Christ.*"

So, the Kingdom of Heaven is the Melchizedek's Kingdom. It is spiritual and entered into by righteousness. Possessed by faith and maintained by love, this kingdom guarantees peace and joy.

Chapter 7 - Royal Law

Genesis 1:26 "And God said, 'Let us make man in our image, after our likeness, and let them have dominion over the fish of the sea, and over the fowl of the air, and over the cattle, and overall, the earth...."

Genesis 1:28 "And God blessed them, and God said unto them, 'Be fruitful, and multiply, and replenish the earth, and subdue it, and have dominion over the fish of the sea, and over the fowl of the air, and over every living thing that moves upon the earth."

Genesis 2:8 "And the Lord God planted a garden eastward in Eden, and there he put the man whom he had formed."

Genesis 2:15 "And the Lord God took the man and put him into the garden of Eden to dress it and to keep it."

In the beginning, Adam was given dominion. Dominion, or *radah*, means to tread under, to subjugate. This, in effect, meant none possessed more authority than he in the realm of *'erets*, that is other than Yahweh. And because that was so, he was to "tread" upon all who contended with him.

Genesis 1:26 according to Young's Literal Translation: *"And God saith, 'Let Us make man in Our image, according to Our likeness, <u>and let them rule</u> over fish of the sea, and over fowl of the heavens, and over cattle, <u>and overall, the earth</u>, and over every creeping thing that is creeping on the earth.'"*

The "them" of the previous verse was both Adam and Eve. Eve was given to Adam for the precise reason stated in Genesis 2: She was to "help" him as he went forth to establish his authority.

Clearly, Adam was assigned to govern 'erets as a king with absolute sovereignty. The fact that Yahweh created him as the "image and likeness" of himself underscores that truth. Note the Hebrew terms Moses used. Tselem and demuwth suggest Adam represented Yahweh and functioned as "God's mirror image." That is also why Adam is later referred to as the son of God.

Webster's Dictionary defines justice as the quality of being just, righteous, equitable, enforcing the law. That then makes "justice and righteousness" interchangeable terms.

Yahweh rules the cosmos with absolute control! His throne, which he established upon the foundation of justice, guarantees righteousness shall ultimately prevail. Thus, it can be rightfully surmised that the law by which God rules the cosmos secures righteousness.

That leads to the understanding that the King of Righteousness reigns in union with the God of Righteousness. And that the law supporting their kingdom, the Melchizedek Kingdom, establishes the Melchizedek's dominion, thereby guaranteeing righteousness. So, the set of rules (the law) they use to measure righteousness is royal!

Now note the following verses:

1 John 4:8, "He who does not love does not know God, for God is love."

John 3:16, "For God so loved the cosmos he gave his only begotten Son...."

James 2:8, *"If you really fulfill the* <u>*royal law*</u> *according to the Scripture, 'You shall* <u>*love*</u> *your neighbor as yourself,' you do well…."*

Do you see the connection? God gave the cosmos the King of Righteousness – to establish the rule of righteousness so that HIS love will be made manifest.

That we might distinguish the law of the kingdom from the law given to Moses, I borrowed the term "royal law" from James 2:8.

Royal is *basilikos* in Koine Greek. Simply stated, *basilikos* refers to the belongings of a sovereign.

James also referred to this law as being perfect. *"But the man who looks intently into the* <u>*perfect* </u>*law that gives freedom, and continues to do this, not forgetting what he has heard, but doing it - he will be blessed in what he does,"* James 1:25.

Teleious (perfect) means complete, fully matured. Thus, the Royal Law is absolute and lacks nothing; it is the Law of Love.

Mark 12:28-34, *"Then one of the scribes came, and having heard them reasoning together, perceiving that He had answered them well, asked Him, 'Which is the first commandment of all?'*

"Jesus answered him, 'The first of the commandments is: Hear, O Israel, the Lord our God, the Lord is one. And you shall love the Lord your God with all your heart, with all your soul, with all your mind, and with all your strength. This is the first commandment. And the second, like it, is this: You shall love your neighbor as yourself. There is no other commandment greater than these.'

"So, the scribe said to Him, 'Well said, Teacher. You have spoken the truth, for there is one God, and there is no other but He. And to love Him with all the heart, with all the understanding, with all the soul, and with all the strength, and to love one's neighbor as oneself, is more than all the whole burnt offerings and sacrifices.'

"Now, when Jesus saw that he answered wisely, He said to him, 'You are not far from the kingdom of God.' But after that, no one dared question Him."

Deuteronomy 6:4-5: *"Hear, O Israel: The Lord our God, the Lord is one. Love the Lord your God with all your heart and with all your soul and with all your strength."*

Yeshua connected these verses in Deuteronomy to Leviticus 19:18, *"Do not seek revenge or bear a grudge against one of your people but love your neighbor as yourself. I am the Lord."*

The rabbi, with whom the Lord spoke, did the same. He even expounded by saying the two commandments were more imperative to follow than the ones concerning burnt offerings and sacrifices. His statement was profound, considering the scribe was not a disciple of Yeshua's. According to Matthew's rendering of this same story, the rabbi was a Pharisee lawyer.

As a strict follower of Moses' law, the rabbi would have known that the Pharisees centered their worship around temple offerings and sacrifices. Especially placing a great value on the *olah* of the burnt sacrifice.

Olah is that which ascends, that which goes up in smoke. The *olah* signified submission. So, commendably, the rabbi stated that when Yahweh "sees" love in action, he is moved, more so than by the *olah* of a sacrifice. He concluded that love represents an inward commitment, whereas the *olah* is an outward show.

Noting the rabbi's wisdom, Yeshua responded by saying, *"You are not far from Yahweh's kingdom."*

Yeshua did not say the rabbi had entered the kingdom of God but that he was near to it.

Yeshua was hinting at the greater truth. The Levitical system only pointed to the kingdom of God. To be in the kingdom of God, one must be in obedience to the Royal Law – they must love.

Sue Watkins

Chapter 8 – Emmaus Road

Luke 24:13-49, "Now behold, two of them were traveling that same day to a village called Emmaus, which was seven miles from Jerusalem. And they talked together of all these things which had happened. So it was, while they conversed and reasoned, that Jesus Himself drew near and went with them. But their eyes were restrained so that they did not know Him. And He said to them, 'What kind of conversation is this that you have with one another as you walk and are sad?' Then the one whose name was Cleopas answered and said to Him, 'Are You the only stranger in Jerusalem, and have You not known the things which happened there in these days?' And He said to them, 'What things?' So, they said to Him, 'The things concerning Jesus of Nazareth, who was a Prophet mighty in deed and word before God and all the people, and how the chief priests and our rulers delivered Him to be condemned to death and crucified Him. But we were hoping that it was He who was going to redeem Israel. Indeed, besides all this, today is the third day since these things happened. Yes, and certain women of our company, who arrived at the tomb early, astonished us. When they did not find His body, they came saying that they had also seen a vision of angels who said He was alive. And certain of those who were with us went to the tomb and found it just as the women had said, but Him they did not see.' Then He said to them, 'O foolish ones, and slow of heart to believe in all that the prophets have spoken!

Ought not the Christ to have suffered these things and to enter into His glory?' And beginning at Moses and all the Prophets, He expounded to them in all the Scriptures the things concerning Himself. "Then they drew near to the village where they were going, and He indicated that He would have gone farther. But they constrained Him, saying, 'Abide with us, for it is toward evening, and the day is far spent.' And He went in to stay with them. Now it came to pass, as He sat at the table with them, that He took bread, blessed, and broke it, and gave it to them. Then their eyes were opened, and they knew Him, and He vanished from their sight. And they said to one another, 'Did not our heart burn within us while He talked with us on the road, and while He opened the Scriptures to us?' So, they rose up that very hour and returned to Jerusalem and found the eleven and those who were with them gathered together, saying, 'The Lord is risen indeed, and has appeared to Simon!' And they told about the things that had happened on the road and how He was known to them in the breaking of bread.*

"Now as they said these things, Jesus Himself stood in the midst of them, and said to them, 'Peace to you. But they were terrified and frightened and supposed they had seen a spirit. And He said to them, 'Why are you troubled? And why do doubts arise in your hearts? Behold My hands and My feet, that it is I Myself. Handle Me and see, for a spirit does not have flesh and bones as you see I have.'*

When He had said this, He showed them His hands and His feet. But while they still did not believe for joy and marveled, He said to them, 'Have you any food here?' So, they gave Him a piece of broiled fish and some honeycomb. And He took it and ate in their presence.

"Then He said to them, 'These are the words which I spoke to you while I was still with you, that all things must be fulfilled which were written in the <u>Law of Moses</u> (Torah) <u>and the Prophets and the Psalms concerning Me.</u>' And He opened their understanding, <u>that they might comprehend the Scriptures</u>. Then He said to them, 'Thus it is written, and thus <u>it was necessary for the Christ</u> (Messiah Melchizedek) <u>to suffer and to rise from the dead the third day, and that repentance and remission of sins should be preached in His name to all nations, beginning at Jerusalem</u>. And you are witnesses of these things. Behold, I send the Promise of My Father upon you; but tarry in the city of Jerusalem until you are endued with power from on high.'" NKJV

When praying about how best to summarize this manuscript, I kept hearing *Emmaus*. So, I meditated upon Luke 24, hoping for insight. But nothing sprang to mind. At least not regarding Jesus as the Melchizedek. Then suddenly, it dawned upon me that this story is all about how Jesus clarified that Scripture, beginning with Genesis 1, foretold his coming. Not as the Messiah, the Son of God, or the Son of Man, but as the Eternal King. For he, as the Melchizedek, is the Anointed One who is both Son of God and Son of Man.

He opened their understanding of Scripture with Moses's words starting with Genesis, moved to the Psalms, and concluded with the Prophets.

Please allow me the pleasure of doing something similar. First, however, note the backdrop of what was happening. Cleopas and his friend, both followers of Yeshua of Nazareth, departed Jerusalem after the Passover to make the seven-mile journey to Emmaus.

Like many others, they followed Yeshua's ministry because he performed unexplainable miracles and raised the dead. Yeshua spoke with such authority that even the elements, as well as demons, obeyed him.

The people's hope rose because Yeshua appeared to be the promised Messiah. All indicators caused them to believe Yeshua was the one whom the prophets said would be sent by Yahweh.

However, just as they began to accept him as the one who was promised, the Passover crucifixion happened. Once again, they were robbed of hope. Disheartened, the two friends traveled home.

So, let's imagine their conversation. It might have gone like this: Cleopas walked some distance in pensive silence before saying, "I recall hearing Yeshua say once, 'The Son of Man must be delivered into the hands of sinful men, be crucified, and the third day he shall rise again.' Perhaps, I shouldn't be surprised he was crucified, yet I am."

"It is all so perplexing." Cleopas' friend retorted. "Where's his body if he is dead? If he is not, why hasn't he appeared to someone? I mean, his disciples wouldn't steal his body. What could they do with it? Not only would hiding his body be disrespectful to his memory, but the thought of finding a hiding place for a decaying body is ridiculous. The Romans and the members of the Sanhedrin are lying to everyone. It is they who must have taken his body."

Cleopas shrugging his shoulders while tossing his hands in the air, exclaimed, "I don't know what to believe anymore!"

Just at that moment, a stranger drew near. He came alongside the two friends and immediately noted their downcast faces. He asked if all was all right.

Cleopas quickly explained why they were sad. Then Yeshua replied, "Obviously, you do not understand Scripture. Not only is your faith in the Anointed One slow, so is your mind. It is dull, for these things were necessary. The Anointed One came to suffer that he might receive the glory due to him as the Son of God.

"Since you have so little understanding, let's examine the intent of what was written. If you recall, the Prophet Isaiah said of the Anointed One he would come up of the dry ground as a tender plant. That he would be rejected and despised, a man of sorrows. Yet he would be wounded for the transgressions of men and be bruised for their iniquities. Your Yeshua of Nazareth never opened his mouth, and it was as Isaiah wrote, he was led as a lamb to slaughter.

"According to Leviticus, without the shedding of blood, there is no remission of sin. Abraham said to his son, Isaac, *'Yahweh shall provide for himself a lamb'*- so you see the Messiah must be a Lamb. Yeshua came as a lamb – not as a lion.

"He came to be the sacrifice for the removal of sin. The world must be redeemed - bought back from the Spirit of Death. Then, it can once again become the sanctuary of Yahweh. Just as it was when Adam ruled and reigned.

"Let me ask you, what was the reason Yahweh called out to Abraham? Instructing him to leave Ur and make his way back to this land. Was it not to make him *l'goy'* - a nation of people through which all people were to be blessed? Yahweh made an example of Abraham – he caused him to be both a type and a pathway.

"Abraham typified Yahweh. Especially when offering Isaac, his son of promise, upon an altar. Yet, he also became a pathway. Yahweh used him 'to father' HIS Kingdom.

"One of the psalmists wrote, '*I have set my King on my holy hill of Zion. I will declare the decree you are my Son, and I have begotten you. Ask of me, and I will give you the nations for your inheritance and the ends of the earth for your possession.*'

"So, God brought forth his Son and offered him on the Cross at Passover. Yeshua died as the Lamb of God. He rose as the King established on the hill of Zion, but not to reign as king but to rule as High Priest. Yeshua must redeem his inheritance as a High Priest.

"For in another place, it was written: '*Remember your congregation, which You have purchased of old, the tribe of your inheritance, which You have redeemed — this Mount Zion where You have dwelt. Lift up Your feet to the perpetual desolations. The enemy has damaged everything in the sanctuary. Your enemies roar in the midst of Your meeting place; they set up their banners for signs.*'

"The damage that verse speaks of is Adam's sin. His disobedience effectively opened up a pathway unto the fallen gods giving them a measure of influence over humanity.

"The true sanctuary of Yahweh is the heart, the soul, of man. So, the enemies of Yahweh deceived Adam, and then Noah inadvertently compounded the problem. He allowed the adversary to build a counter kingdom, which only worsened the situation and further corrupted the destiny of mankind. Remember Nimrod? He constructed the Tower of Babel and implemented a false system of government.

"However, like the Tower of Babel, these things must fall to the ground and be scattered to the wind. But first, men's hearts must be recaptured, or they will continue to build without regard to Yahweh.

"People, all people, no matter where they live, exist in a spiritual Egypt. Egypt typifies Nimrod's false system. The whole world needs an Exodus experience that they might know Yahweh.

"For that reason, Yahweh gave Abraham a son in his old age – a son of promise. Through Isaac and his descendants, Yahweh promised to restore all which was forfeited by Adam and Noah.

"Regarding that promise, we must not forget that Adam was created as the immortal king of 'erets. That was the reason Eve was promised a Seed. Which meant the Seed had to be like Adam, both God's son and a man. Additionally, he would have to possess all authority.

"In other words, the Promised Seed needed to have a Divine nature, which afforded him the necessary authority to command the spirit world. And he must have the right to sit on Adam's throne.

"The Promised One must have the qualifications, which means the lineage, which gives him the right to rule as king over all the kings of the earth, eternally.

"But none of Adam's descendants could do that. How could they? They, like he, were subject to the spirit of death. Therefore, two requirements were placed upon the Promised Seed. First, he must obtain, legally, the Melchizedek throne, then he must triumph over Death.

"So you see, the Messiah had to die. But his death is not the end. It is the beginning of restoration to Yahweh's prophesied kingdom.

"Of course, Jerusalem and indeed all of Israel shall be redeemed. Did Zechariah not write, 'And the Lord will take possession of Judah as His inheritance in the Holy Land and will again choose Jerusalem.'

However, it is also written, 'Many nations shall be joined to the Lord in that day, and they shall become My people. And I will dwell in your midst. Then you will know that the Lord of hosts has sent Me to you.'

"Daniel also prophesied that this kingdom Yahweh establishes shall be forever. He wrote: '*And in the days of these kings the God of heaven will set up a kingdom which shall never be destroyed, and the kingdom shall not be left to other people; it shall break in pieces and consume all these kingdoms, and it shall stand forever.*'

"Isaiah wrote: '*For unto us a Child is born, unto us a Son is given, and the government will be upon his shoulder... of the increase of his government and peace there will be no end. Upon the throne of David and over his kingdom, order it and establish it with judgment and justice from that time forward, even forever. The zeal of the Lord of hosts will perform this.'*

"Yahweh has set in place an order, the order of Melchizedek. Adam was its first king, but he was temporal. Yahweh knew Adam would die.

"Death is a tool in the hands of the adversaries. They use it, hoping to slow the progression of the Kingdom of God. The demonic seek to draw mankind into death, thinking they can separate humanity from Yahweh, thus foil the plan of redemption.

"That is why Yahweh laid upon Yeshua the punishment of evil – why he was made the sin offering. He was put to death so that all might live.

"As the psalmist predicted, his soul was poured out like water before Death. But Yeshua is no longer in the Pit. He has risen."

Yeshua continued to teach them. Still, they did not recognize that it was Yeshua who spoke until they decided to eat their evening meal. When he broke the bread that they shared, their eyes were opened, and they knew him.

Revelation 3:20-21, *"Behold, I stand at the door and knock. If anyone hears My voice and opens the door, I will come into him and dine with him, and he with Me. To him who overcomes I will grant to sit with Me on My throne, as I also overcame and sat down with My Father on His throne."*

Hebrews 7:25, *"Wherefore he is able also to save them to the uttermost that come unto God by him, seeing he ever lives to make intercession for them."*

John 1:14, *"And the Word became flesh and dwelt (tent or tabernacle) among us, and we beheld His glory, the glory as of the only begotten of the Father, full of grace and truth."*

Glory or *doxa,* as used in this verse, is a noun. It means <u>dignity and</u> honor.

John 4:23-24, *"But the hour is coming, and now is, when the <u>true worshipers will worship the Father in spirit and truth</u>; for the Father is seeking such to worship Him. God is Spirit, and <u>those who worship Him must worship in spirit and truth</u>."*

1 John 5:10-12, *"Anyone who believes in the Son of God has this testimony in his heart. Anyone who does not believe God has made him out to be a liar because he has not believed the testimony God has given about his Son. <u>And this is the testimony: God has given us eternal life, and this life is in his Son. He who has the Son has life; he who does not have the Son of God does not have life</u>."*

Isaiah 61:1-4, *"The Spirit of the Lord God is upon me; because the Lord hath anointed me to preach good tidings unto the meek; he hath sent me to bind up the brokenhearted, to proclaim liberty to the captives, and the opening of the prison to them that are bound; to proclaim the acceptable year of the Lord, and the day of vengeance of our God; to comfort all that mourn; to appoint unto them that mourn in Zion, <u>to give unto them beauty for ashes, the oil of joy for mourning, the garment of praise for the spirit of heaviness; that they might be called trees of righteousness</u>, the planting of the Lord, that he might be glorified. And they shall build the old wastes, they shall raise up the former desolations, <u>and they shall repair the waste cities, the desolations of many generations.</u>"*

Hebrews 5:9-11, "...*and having been perfected, He became the author of eternal salvation to all who obey Him, called by God as High Priest 'according to the order of Melchizedek,' of whom we have much to say, and hard to explain....*"

Matthew 11:25-30, "*At that time Jesus answered and said, 'I thank You, Father, Lord of heaven and earth, that You have hidden these things from the wise and prudent and have revealed them to babes. Even so, Father, for so it seemed good in Your sight.' All things have been delivered to Me by My Father, and no one knows the Son except the Father. Nor does anyone know the Father except the Son, and the one whom the Son will reveal Him. Come to Me, all you who labor and are heavy laden, and I will give you rest. Take My yoke upon you and learn from Me, for I am gentle and lowly in heart, and you will find rest for your souls. For my yoke is easy, and my burden is light.*"

Made in the USA
Middletown, DE
21 May 2022

66058011R00076